Praise for **INVISIBLE CHILDREN**

It is truly critical for adults from all corners of our society to speak out on behalf of children, especially children without someone who cares about them and their futures. Mike Tikkanen's book takes a very hard look at what is happening to some of those very special children and the adults they become. His work and the work of thousands of guardians ad-Litem mean life or death to children whose needs depend on "the system" and the court. I deeply appreciate Mike's willingness to say what needs to be said.

—Connie Skillingstad,
Executive Director,
Prevent Child Abuse Minnesota

In his book, *Invisible Children*, Mike Tikkanen writes with passion as he advocates for protecting children from the toxic environments of abusive homes. He constantly urges the reader to get involved in providing a better world for the most vulnerable in American society.

—Tom Daly, Regional Teacher of the
Year; Educational Administrator,
MN Dept of Corrections

Mike's book tells of his experiences helping children as a guardian ad-Litem. He encourages everyone to become aware of what needs to change. We can all do small things to make children's lives better. After you read his book, you'll be asking yourself, "What can I do

:her,
:her,
ther

D1509597

All children are born into a promise that the adults in their lives would take care of them. Unfortunately, that promise all too often gets broken and the only recourse these children have is a Child Protection System and Juvenile Justice System that certainly could use more help. It is my hope the stories and arguments in this book will be a first step in our recommitment to all of our children.

—Senator (State of MN) Mee Moua

Having adopted four older children that have experienced the effects of abuse, neglect on children, and the workings of the foster care system, I have come to realize all the love in the world will not "fix broken children." Saying we care about children is not enough; we need to read this book and be proactive in the fight for all children. Mike Tikkanen tells it like it is! He is committed to making a difference. Are you willing to join him?

—Patti Hetrick, Adoptive Mother

Open your ears to riveting and accurate stories of today's children. Mike's eye opening experiences encourage us all to reach out and make life better for troubled children in our communities.

—Donald Schmitz, Author and
Founder of The Grandkidsandme
Foundation

I just read your book from start to finish. I want to congratulate you for what is a very POWERFUL message. Its readability is excellent and the unfolding of the story is gripping, even gut-wrenching.

—David Strand, Guardian ad-Litem;
Author, *Nation Out of Step*

INVISIBLE CHILDREN

Preteen Mothers, Adolescent Felons
& What We Can Do About It

TIKKANEN

Andover, Minnesota

ISBN 13: 978-1-931945-34-9
ISBN 10: 1-931945-34-9

Library of Congress Catalog Number: 2005925593

Printed in the United States of America

First Printing: June 2005

08 07 06 05 04   5 4 3 2 1

Andover,
Minnesota

Expert Publishing, Inc.
14314 Thrush Street NW,
Andover, MN 55304-3330
1-877-755-4966
www.expertpublishinginc.com

This book is dedicated to the thousands of voiceless children who, born into terrifying circumstances and suffering through the unexplainable pain of abuse and neglect, find themselves in America's Child Protection Systems each year.

By helping others, we help ourselves. Learning and understanding are worthwhile goals.

What we do to our children
they will do to society.

Pliny the Elder

TABLE OF CONTENTS

FOREWORD

Mike Tikkanen's book, *Invisible Children*, is an urgent call to action which describes, in plain, heart-wrenching terms, how our institutions act as enablers of child abuse. He outlines how America's current strategies and institutions are being overwhelmed by the magnitude and severity of the problem of child abuse. I would take it a step further and say that his book is an indictment of the very institutions we have established to protect the weakest among us: our children.

It is not teachers, school administrators, social workers, police, or therapists causing the problems in our schools, communities, and prisons. These hard-working, well-intentioned professionals are not to blame. As he correctly points out, they are doing the best they can within the framework of laws, regulations, and policies. The issue he brings to light is much broader and much deeper. It is not an issue of blame—of "right versus wrong." It is an issue of "right versus right," the very definition of tragedy.

In 1994, I completed a study extending over five years[1] and concluded that certain human service agencies and law enforcement services designed to solve such problems as crime, illiteracy, child abuse, drug addiction, poverty, and homelessness

1. Long, Kathleen S. "Dancing with Demons: Pathogenic Problem Solving Systems." PhD diss., The Fielding Graduate Institute, Santa Barbara, California. 1994.

actually operate within a hidden inherent logic to perpetuate and exacerbate the very conditions they were designed to cure. Put differently, the purpose of any system is what it does. What the Child Protection System does is produce victims and future inmates for the Criminal Justice System.

Generation after generation, these abused children fill our prisons, overwhelm our schools, and make our cities unsafe for the people who must live in them. Our current policies ensure more crime and prisons, failing schools, and a growing number of neighborhoods unfit for human habitation.

There are no simple answers to these problems. However, this I know. These problems cannot be solved within the framework of the current system that created them. More programs, new laws, and additional regulations will only produce a temporary remission before there is a rebound and escalation of the original problem.

This is a hard hitting, often uncomfortable, book about an enormous, complicated, and painful problem. Mike Tikkanen has taken a courageous stand to open our eyes and expose the truth. It is now up to all of us to confront the truth and begin this essential dialogue.

—Kathleen S. Long, PhD
April, 2005

ACKNOWLEDGMENTS

First and foremost, my wife, Cathy, for her patience and kindness when this project has proved burdensome.

To those who work with abused and neglected children as teachers, social workers, foster and adoptive parents, and service providers. It is with your great efforts that abused and neglected children can become normal happy people.

Harry and Sharron Stockhausen at Expert Publishing, Inc., I appreciate your knowledge and patient approach to getting this book completed in a professional manner.

Norm Stoehr, Damon Kocina, A.J. Meyer, Dave Hobza, Bob Olson, Linc Shea, David Strand, Russ Hagen, my Inner Circle supporters and friends have all gone the extra mile to help make this book and my larger efforts possible.

To Susanne Smith, Marti Swanson, Christine Johnson, and all of you at the guardian ad-Litem program whose diligent daily efforts help children to have a voice in their own lives.

Thanks to Connie Anderson for her ability to help me organize and conceptualize this book in its initial stages, for clarifying and give me direction by her first-draft edit, and for her energy and efforts to launch the book.

To everyone who cares enough about the weakest and most vulnerable among us to make an effort to improve the lives of abandoned and neglected children.

Thank you.

PREFACE

The writing of this book took about eight months. However the data and statistics appearing within it were compiled over twenty years. The book may be criticized for including information gathered over those years. I would argue that the bigger story being told here is the evolution of American social policy in my lifetime. It was not my intention to write an academic work or a tome of current statistical data. In most instances, the data has remained about the same for twenty years.

Historically, America has compared itself to the other twenty industrialized nations of the world. Those are the nations with 50–200-year-old democracies we have seen as our equals and wanted to use to define how we ranked in the world: Japan, Germany, France, Great Britain, Italy, Canada, Australia, Netherlands, Belgium, Sweden, Austria, Switzerland, Israel, Denmark, Finland, Norway, New Zealand, Ireland, Iceland.

For the last twenty years, America has fallen from the top to the bottom in many of the quality-of-life comparisons with the other industrialized nations.

Whether measuring child literacy, poverty, per-capita rates of crime and incarceration, lifting children out of poverty, health care, or a broad range of social comparisons, America has lost its leading position in the industrialized world.

Rather than honestly addressing this steep decline, information providers and the media have started to include the "emerging" nations in quality-of-life comparisons. This shows America in the middle of the forty-three emerging nations rather than at the bottom of the well-established and more meaningful industrialized nations' contrast. To compare our nation with Botswana—because we are unable to compete internationally with other industrialized nations—is a failure we need to wake up to.

We are hiding our poor performance in critical quality-of-life issues by claiming we rank in the middle of forty-three developing nations. It would be more honest and meaningful to acknowledge our last-place status in the industrialized world, and work to change it, than to lower our standards and accept Third-World status for education, health care, poverty, and in so many other areas.

This book is a simple recruitment effort to get the average person to speak for and become friends of children.

www.friendsofchildren.com

www.invisiblechildren.org

Before I became a guardian ad-Litem, I spent a year with failing third graders as a volunteer reader at a local grade school. It was light duty and satisfying to experience improvements in reading skills for the tiny investment in time per child. A few hours a month with a volunteer reader makes literate children out of failing third graders. What a rewarding program for both the child and volunteer.

I became aware of the guardian ad-Litem program at the same time a close friend (Pam) was experiencing serious problems with a local county Child Protection System. My friend was not told of the severe abuse and mental health issues, or the serious behavioral problems, of the three children her family had adopted. Pam and her husband had, in fact, adopted three very troubled children from a county that told them nothing of the tortured homes these children had spent their lives in.

The county became unreasonable, evasive, and dishonest once the adoption was finalized. I watched for several years as Pam tried to make her small business run and lead a normal life while living with the impossible problems her abused and neglected children were plagued by.

County agencies treated Pam and her family badly. As a result, they have all suffered terrific unnecessary stress for many years. Pam's children did not receive mental health treatments that could have helped them deal with their severe and chronic problems. Because a government agency chose not to disclose the truth about the abuse and neglect of her adopted children, those children could not receive timely mental health services.

It has taken many years for Pam and her children to sort through their problems and deal with the issues that so dramatically affect their quality of life as individuals and as a family. This county's behavior has had a lasting impact on the view I have of under-funded and misdirected government agencies.

Invisible Children represents years of my research into children's issues and my own experiences with children in the Child Protection System. I do not speak for all abused and neglected children everywhere. I admit to a personal bias for children born into miserable lives. They have suffered enough.

I am hurt by the meanness and shortsightedness of the politics that are drowning these children.

Eight years ago I volunteered as a child advocate within my county's Child Protection System. I have worked with about fifty Invisible Children and become very close to some of them. I call them *Invisible* because they are hidden from our community—and they cannot escape their circumstances without our help. They are not heard or seen until they do something terrible which prompts our society to abuse them all over again.

Child Protection workers might become desensitized to eleven-year-old abused girls sneaking out of group homes to seduce men at a nearby bar, but it made me crazy. I don't want my community to facilitate the abandonment of abused children a second time.

My observations may not be right in every application, but most of my positions have been born out in the research I have done. You may dislike what you see and disagree with my positions, but the facts have been the facts for many years.

None of the following information can be considered a one-year anomaly. It disturbs me to know that most of the data and statistics in this book have been true for about twenty years. It also hurts me to think that many of my friends and most of my political acquaintances know very little about this important information.

I'm a skinny, fifty-ish, entrepreneurial, happily married, and optimistic guy who runs a small business and likes to experience new things. I've owned a junkyard and crushed car bodies, been a travelling salesman, business consultant, and a recruiter for a private school.

I've won and lost, reinvented myself, done fairly well, and done poorly. I'm living proof that this country is home to a multitude of possibilities for unconventional lifestyles that allow many of us the opportunity to discover the things we love and build them into a life that is rich and fulfilling (with the right help).

I'm a lucky guy and I know it. Eight years of working with unlucky babies, three-year-olds, and seven-year-old children, has shown me how lucky I am.

The difference between lucky and unlucky is what prompts me to write this book. I am lucky because my mom loved me and kept me from harm. We were a broken family with alcohol, divorce, and money problems.

What's important here, though, is that she instilled in me the belief that *life is good* and that you can *trust* some people most of the time (and you can trust most people a little).

This may be simple and obvious as the nose on your face—unless you come from a family that abused and neglected you. Then you might not think life is good or that you should ever trust *anybody*.

Take Nancy, who at six was the oldest of four children of a crack cocaine mom. Nancy and her family lived with an abusive man who liked to have sex with children. Nancy was sexually and physically abused by this man for four years, and was once kicked so hard by him that she went into convulsions.

After repeated police calls to the home by neighbors, Nancy and her siblings were finally discovered by Child Protection and removed from their home. Parental rights were terminated, and the children were adopted into other families.

That is, except for Nancy, eleven years old, too troubled, too explosive, and too self-loathing to allow herself to be loved, or even cared for by sweet decent people.

Nationally, four years is the average length of time for sexual abuse of a child within a toxic family before they are removed.

Children are not aware of the rightness or wrongness of their abuse. They do not know that abuse is abnormal, or even that it is wrong. To a three-year-old, no matter how painful and frightening her life is, her life *is* normal. A sad and lasting fact of child abuse is that children blame themselves for the abuse they receive. It takes years of therapy to change a child's perception of an abusive past.

There is no book a child can go to, or code they are born with, that explains the abnormality of what is happening to them. Children can't call their senators, or complain to the authorities (they can't even tell their parents).

Abused children cope as best they can. Abused kids develop behaviors that work against them for the *rest of their lives* (as I will explain). Their behaviors will define them as social misfits and prompt them to do things that will make the rest of their lives miserable.

While these children are invisible to most of our community, each one of us is directly responsible for their plight. They live under our laws; they go to our schools; they are convicted by our courts; many of them spend lifetimes in our prisons. They have no say in the laws and policies that rule their lives. And if they did, they are too young to know what to say. So, as responsible adults who make the laws, each of us must begin to stand up for these children.

If we don't, who will?

ONE

Alex

(*The Cost of Money Saved*)

If freedom means anything, it is the right to tell people what they do not want to hear.

—*George Orwell*

- Ninety percent of the juveniles in the Juvenile Justice System have come out of the Child Protection System (Minnesota's Chief Justice, Kathleen Blatz). Over 90 percent of the adults in the Criminal Justice System come out of the Juvenile Justice System. Justice Blatz (and others) call it a prison "feeder" system.

- The United States is *the only nation in the world* to build prisons based on failed third grade reading scores (Arizona and California; David Strand, *Nation out of Step*, p. 93).

- Nationally, *over* 50 percent of incarcerated youth have diagnosable mental illness. (Children's Defense Fund,

2001.) These are mental conditions that cause behaviors that condemn children to poor and unhappy lives on the edges of society. Treated, these children can learn to cope and meld into society. Untreated mental illness is responsible for many of the problems being experienced within American schools, courts, and communities. Abused and neglected children and their mental health issues will continue to make headlines and terrorize our communities until we decide to solve the problem.

A guardian ad-Litem is a court-appointed advocate for children in the Child Protection System. I have been a guardian for about fifty children over eight years. These are my observations and stories about my guardian ad-Litem children and information that I believe is important for all Americans, but especially the children.

My young friend Alex is a slight, sweet boy who has real gifts for music and dance. With no help or training, he placed second out of 1100 children at his high school talent show with an amazing dance routine. Alex is smart, too.

Had the state left Alex in the foster home where he was placed at birth, he could have led a normal suburban life with decent parents and loving siblings. His birth mom had lost two other children to Child Protection due to her cocaine addiction. Alex was born cocaine positive and came to live with a happy and caring family in a warm and inviting home.

At fifteen, he should have been thinking about normal teen things, instead of living in his twenty-seventh foster care placement in seven years.

Instead, he lives with constant anxiety and fear from the four frightful years he was locked in a bedroom days at a time, starved, tied to a bed, sexually abused, and beaten by his demented father. Can you imagine a four-year-old boy being tied to a bed and left alone without food for days at a time? When dad came home, he beat and sexually molested his helpless son.

Alex's mom had her parental rights terminated by the courts. Biological dad petitioned the Minnesota courts for his parental rights to his child. Alex's guardian state did not check with the Wisconsin courts. The Wisconsin court order that forbade the father to be around young boys, because of his criminal sexual history with children, was not discovered until after the four years of violence and sex abuse had occurred.

Both Alex's father and mother have spent most of their lives in the Judicial System. Their parole officers explained to me how both parents had spent most of their adult lives in prison. Neither one of Alex's parents were capable of dealing with the outside world or their own asocial and criminal behaviors. Each of them came out of horrific, toxic homes themselves, passing problems from generation to generation.

It is a common error (or policy) that state courts have not been motivated to cooperate with other state courts in these matters. The state may not have enough funding to handle its own state internal affairs, let alone worry about the problems another state may be having. In Alex's case, the state would have saved millions of dollars and many years of a child's suffering if it had just spent the few dollars and investigated his biological father's criminal court records.

Perhaps each state believes that it is serving its citizens and saving money by not sharing information. Whatever the rationale, the costs incurred by the state of Minnesota for a child like Alex are very high, and we are by no means done paying. Placements, courts, and therapy, not to mention the suffering of Alex and all the people he affects every day, will continue to cost the state until he has learned coping skills, and sufficiently unlearned his early childhood lessons.

Like so many abused and neglected state ward children, Alex did not receive the help he needs for his severe and chronic problems, and he will spend many years suffering because of it.

There is also a cost to the mayhem damaged children cause the people they encounter. Neglected and abused children make up a great majority of the crime, drugs, and violence we see on TV and in our newspapers.

We all know how valuable it is to simply feel safe and know that our own family members are not endangered. We know how terrible it is when that illusion is dashed and one of our own is robbed, murdered, or raped.

Alex knows he's not normal. He would so like to be normal, but he doesn't know where to start. If he were normal, he wouldn't be ridiculed in school and among his peers, a failure in school, and neurotic (and sometimes psychotic) when dealing with authority figures who try to make him do things like conform or follow the rules.

Some of us view the parents of neglected and abused children as irresponsible, violent, or addicted and find it possible to blame them and forget about it. This solves nothing. We will either understand and address the problem or it will get worse.

It's critical to realize parents with severe underlying psychiatric disorders and chronic and damaging drug and alcohol addictions create a home life that guarantees their children a terrifying childhood. This creates a child as dysfunctional as the parent, who will go on to create his or her own dysfunctional family. It's a cycle that rarely ends without intervention.

When biological dad finally placed Alex in school (at the age of seven), the first observant nurse saw the big bruises all over his body and did the right thing. Within a short time, Alex was placed in foster care and Child Protection was able to wrest custody from the father.

Traumatic living conditions and physical assaults have had a monstrous impact on Alex's development as a human being. His abuse was not singular or occasional, but repeated regularly over many years. Human behaviors change to meet the demands of the environment. In this developmental respect, all sentient beings are alike. Staying alive and avoiding pain becomes hardwired into mental circuitry. Nothing else matters. Abused children like Alex develop very differently from non-abused children.

Coping behaviors learned by abused children are terribly counter-productive once the child is out of the abusive circumstances and trying to live a normal life. The behaviors developed for staying alive and avoiding pain dominate and thus can become significant detriments to getting along in society. As a matter of fact, for many troubled youth, their explosive responses and pain avoidance behaviors define them as social misfits and send them to prison.

It is impossible to overstate Alex's level of anxiety. Concentration is not a skill owned by any of the abused and neglected children I have known. Hyper-vigilant to his surroundings, untrusting, always seeking, unable to breathe deeply and relax even for a minute, Alex is uncomfortable in almost all situations. His self-loathing is frightening and painful to witness.

For the better part of eight years, I have visited Alex in the many foster and group homes that he has lived in around the state. I have yet to visit a foster home or group home that has the training, amenities, services, or therapies needed to accomplish their complex and difficult tasks. It is my hope that one day my community will provide all group homes with decent furniture, a working piano, and enough trained staff to adequately deal with the exceedingly complicated lives of the children they work with.

I do not wish to diminish the efforts of the committed and caring people who are trying desperately to help these children. My point is that all the facilities are overcrowded and understaffed. Many of the therapists and social workers are young and under-trained for their complex tasks, often in over their heads.

Pay is poor and transfers are common. Neglected and abused children need long-term relationships with adults (any adults). By under-appreciating this fact and under-paying and under-respecting the people who provide the life blood services to these children, our systems ensure there will be no consistency or long-term relationships for children in our Child Protection Systems. All abandoned children have an intensive need for human attachment and a very special need for a relationship with a trusted adult.

Alex may never have had a nice day in his life.

Eight years of life within our system of courts and treatments have cost Alex a normal life and our community a million or more dollars in services. In cases like this, with an adolescent boy or girl, our community has only begun to pay. It's not just the money that we should be concerned with, it's the destroyed lives, unsafe streets, and a reputation as a society that throws away children.

Counties act as if the subsidized care of other people's children should be so undesirable and rotten with scarcity that it deters *those people* from behaving in such a way that puts their children in harm's way to be demolished by the system. It's all very cynical and counterproductive. The strong social desire to punish *those people* can only create more and greater pockets of indescribable suffering. Social policy seems to be the punishment will continue until the morale improves.

Providers of services to children are moved around by policy (certain functions/certain people) and by the fact that providers also will move around to climb their own financial and employment ladder. This is the way the system works and is no reflection on the workers. Because of these policies, I may be the only adult who has remained in Alex's life since he entered the Child Protection System.

Social workers rotate out of his life every few years. Social workers rotate out of the lives of all state ward children (who remain in the system). Abandonment issues and the constant turnover of the adult figures in his life have taught Alex not to get too close to people.

He accepts this fluid change of authority figures as the way his world works. This kind of policy does not help abandoned children learn to build relationships or to understand love or trust. Instead, it ensures that relationships will be transitory and children's abandonment issues will be exacerbated.

After many hours of watching and talking with Alex and other children like him, I repeatedly see how hard it is for them to learn how to love or trust another human being. No spouse, no best friend, and in general, no love for himself. Teaching Invisible Children how to love and respect themselves is a very difficult and important task.

Love is a tough concept to relate in this context. It is the single biggest need in the life of an abandoned child. To not have love for oneself, or others, is only part of the problem. The other part is to not be *able* to have it. Abandoned children often have been so badly damaged that they refuse to allow another human being close to them ever again. Once that happens, love can never be a part of their life. By definition, you can't love someone you are not close to.

Troubled children over the age of twelve are the least likely to be adopted and sometimes don't have the luxury of contact with siblings or other family members. Many don't have any past to connect with and no adult figures they can attach to. These become the impossible cases, where the child is moved from group home to foster home and back to a group home, because of serious problematic behaviors.

If we wonder why gangs provide such a magnetic attraction, this is it. Rules, respect, consistency, pride—it is all right here in the gang. Neglected and abused children are very needy. What happens when they don't have needs met is as serious as the initial abuse that brought them into the system. The results are terrible and long lasting, often for life. To not address this simple basic need is an absolute failure of our system and abdication of our responsibility as a community (as in "we the people who make the laws").

Abandoned children need consistency in their lives once they have been removed from their homes. They need immediate and professional help to keep them from rebelling from a society they know hates them (this perception is their reality). The policies most states have for child wards do not provide consistency, high-quality staffing, or services that are needed to get the results these children must have to stay out of gangs and re-enter society.

I have worked with individual neglected children who have had over one hundred different adults in their lives over a six-year period. Talk about feeling passed around and unwanted in a cold bureaucratic system. These kids are not stupid. In short order, a child accurately deduces what kind of relationship he has with the state. He knows it's an uncaring system. He knows that there is little chance for adoption. He knows the feeling of abandonment (for a second, third, and fourth time).

The kind of help these children need does not lend itself to crowded conditions with very disturbed children battling to get their fair share of a therapist's attention. Abandoned children need relationships that last and people who understand and care about them, with the sincerity and training to make a difference.

Mental health services are not a benevolence that society grants to a mentally ill or emotionally damaged child. From an economic perspective, it is far cheaper to help damaged children heal their wounds and become normal functioning adults than it is to let their mental problems fester until outrage and behavioral problems spill out into the community. They will all too soon become parents—with their own history of drugs, crime, violence, and their very own continued family cycle of child abuse.

If there were a point to reinforce with Invisible Children, it would be to provide them with adequate mental health services and a home and school life they require. Most often, we wait until the child has done something terrible to warrant mental health services, and too many children have become unadoptable in our system.

The combination of removal from the only home they have ever known and the traumas suffered from abuse and neglect demands rigorous and extended mental health therapy. Without swift and sufficient mental health services, these children continue to develop poorly, without healing, without direction or understanding. Taking children out of toxic environments is not enough to save them. They need professional guidance.

The Post-Traumatic Stress syndrome suffered by soldiers and victims of horrible crimes is in some ways similar to the mental health trauma suffered by abused children. The difference between soldiers and children is that children had no *before* to relate to. Like a person who has lost her sight after years of seeing, a once-sighted person can remember the concept of seeing, or the soldier can remember the normal life led before the terrifying events that caused their trauma.

Abused children suffered trauma day after day, year in and year out. They do not have a concept of what *before* was like. They cannot know what normal should be. Normal is abuse; normal is torture; normal is sex, drugs, and pain for five-year-olds.

Long-term therapy is a must for children who have undergone the trauma of abuse and abandonment. To not have adequate services for abandoned children guarantees that their learned responses to torture, fear, loss, and grief will supercede behaviors that could facilitate a functional transition into adulthood.

In times of budget shortages, states cut their budgets for human services, crippling each agency's ability to oversee Child Protection services, nursing homes, mental health, and chemical dependency programs. As this book will argue, states save money by providing sufficient and appropriate services to the people who work and live with Invisible Children. It is my observation that not providing services while the chance of rehabilitation exists is far more costly in tax dollars than doing what is right and necessary could ever be.

Foster and adoptive parents are special people and deserve more help than they are getting. They need better training to understand and manage the behaviors of the troubled children they work with. They are often not told of the serious problems their children suffer from, or, if they are told, the issues are minimized. Overcoming the behavioral problems that so often lead to danger and disruption in the adoptive/foster home takes all the training and information available to parents and children alike.

As we better understand the issues affecting abused and neglected children, positive change will occur. Educate the social workers, the foster parents, and the adoptive parents. Foster and adoptive parents need to know and understand the issues they are dealing with. I have witnessed a county placing an autistic child with an unsuspecting family. I have witnessed a county "planting" a psychotic fourteen-year-old boy into a family of young children without warning the parents.

Some counties are making great strides in making available information and educating workers, parents, and service providers. Other counties and government agencies hide information about their state ward children and behave less than honestly towards foster and adoptive parents.

What are these well-meaning families to do when they discover the children they adopted have serious mental health problems they can't begin to understand or deal with? Counties owe state ward children and the families who adopt them the information that will help them deal with the circumstances they are bringing into their homes.

Many of the families who tried to help Alex made extraordinary efforts to give him love and make him one of their own. But in the end, no one was allowed close enough to hurt him again. He caused his own pain. Alex was forced out of his first long-term placement home because he took a knife to his sibling's toys and frightened his adoptive parents (he was nine). Alex's second adoption attempt failed because he threatened to kill the family's dog.

With each new home disruption, Alex further cements his abnormal definition of self. He knows he's not like you or me. The self-disappointment for one more personal failure is nailed into his being.

Alex's destruction of his relationship with his first and most loving foster home were complete. A combination of psychological problems compounded by sexual identity issues made his behaviors unbearable. With early and adequate therapy, he could have managed his mental health issues and remained with his first family placement. The family loved Alex and wanted him to stay with them. They tried to live with his extreme and escalating behavior problems. In the end, he became a danger to himself and the family. He was made to leave.

The fear and terror a small child like Alex lives with is exemplified by recalling the fear he put into three different foster fathers over a three-year period. Alex weighed no more than seventy-five pounds and the smallest of these fathers was well over twice his size and weight. They never won against a whirling dervish with no fear or love for himself and no control of, or awareness of, his "insane" mode. At twelve, he kicked a public school teacher so hard the teacher was severely injured.

Alex has tried to kill himself on several occasions. He has assaulted teachers, stabbed other children with pens and pencils, cut open furniture and mattresses to hide food, and been a frightened, anxiety-ridden child who behaves poorly most of the time, trusts no one, and hates himself and all forms of authority. To hear a young child speak about self-hatred, feeling abnormal and unloved has been one of the hardest parts of my being a guardian ad-Litem.

It is wrong to blame him for his asocial behavior. It accomplishes nothing to blame any of these children for whom they have become. I would do these things too if I had been assaulted as he was (and so would you).

Outrageous behaviors can be seamless to children with mental health problems—they are not even aware of their actions. Many abused children engage in compulsive behaviors that create serious barriers to being normal. These behaviors control and define abused and neglected children. Normal is something that Alex speaks of and dreams about.

On a busy weekend for suicides, when all juvenile psychiatric hospital beds were filled, Alex was sent out of town for his own safety. The only juvenile psychiatric beds available were at a Christian Group home four hours out of the metro area. The state flew me up with him (as his guardian ad-Litem). I could ask questions, but I had no authority to change anything. The Ph.D. therapist promised me that Alex's sexuality issues would not be a problem.

Funding had recently been cut to this organization and large staff cuts had destroyed morale. Alex gave me permission to speak to the psychologist about his sexuality issues, so I did. She guaranteed me the boy was in good hands with progressive, positive people.

I learned later that this already fragile, suicidal, unhappy boy was scorned, harassed, and ridiculed by the other troubled children for the entire four weeks of his "protective" stay. At the same time, religious staff members tried to convince Alex that Christian doctrine could fix his sexual identity issues. This treatment was wrong for Alex in so many ways. It exemplifies how our social institutions are exacerbating and not solving the problems of neglected and abused children.

I did not see the bills, but this was expensive therapy that resulted in regression to more self-hate, more fear, and more anxiety. Other than keeping Alex from killing himself during his treatment, nothing positive came of his stay. This was not a good use of taxpayer money.

At the same time, there have been many wonderful people who have lived and worked with this boy for his eight years in

Child Protection. Alex has had fourteen case workers, multiple therapists, and a series of miscellaneous county and state workers. He's had perhaps a hundred adults who have worked on his case. No one stays in his life, and no one has been able to undo the damage that was done to him. It would be much more meaningful to Alex, and others like him, if there were some consistency to the adult figures in his life.

If Alex had received adequate psychological counseling after he was removed from his abusive parental home, his behaviors could have been modified to allow him a more normal life. I also believe assigning caseworkers for long term care of state wards (like Alex) would have been helpful for him to learn how to trust adults in his life. Instead, he learned that caseworkers were busy people who would probably be moved from his case and replaced with a new person before too long.

Unwilling or unable to anticipate the initial importance of a basic investigation of the father before granting him custody of Alex, the county and state are spending millions of dollars making this unhappy child into a desperately needy and unhappy juvenile who likely will become a violent and unhappy adult. I know him as a beautiful and gifted child who deserves better.

Did the state think it "unproductive" to take the time or the expense to review the father? Any minor review would have shown a very long criminal file, a judge's order to stay away from young boys, and Alex's dad was in prison when he made the request to gain custody of Alex. Some observers might claim the state had the obligation to look out for the better interests of this child (and really failed in this instance).

In our participatory democracy, are not all of us, as citizens, complicit in Alex's destruction? America is one of the wealthiest and best-educated nations on earth. We have chosen not to see the tens of thousands of Invisible Children living in the same tortured circumstances in the same hopeless cycle of poverty, violence, and incarceration as Alex.

American citizens have chosen the policies that lead to children we don't see not receiving the services they badly need. These children will almost certainly become the next generation of ex-convicts and young mothers having their own families of Invisible Children.

Alex has many times the chance of entering the Juvenile Justice System than your children. For years he has taken psychotropic medications to treat his various mental illnesses. Often, he chooses not to take his medications. Alex has become familiar to police and Juvenile Justice, and I would argue that he is on the verge of discovering the Criminal Justice System.

The price Alex has paid, and has yet to pay, for being born into the wrong family, is a great price indeed.

Alex may or may not become part of the American prison feeder system and one of the six hundred thousand felons released each year. He may become one of the 66 percent of ex-felons who then re-offend and return to prison each year because they do not have the skills to function in our society.

The good news for Alex is that people are trying to help him with his many problems. The bad news is society and the institutions that serve him quickly abandon young men (especially young men of color). Not doing well in school, and being well known to police at a young age, is not a formula for staying out of jail.

Lois, Alex's long-time court-appointed lawyer, and I were talking recently about a system so dysfunctional that she is not contacted when he gets into trouble. Lois, like many other court appointed Child Court attorneys, are volunteers who want to make a difference in the lives of the abused children who become their clients. Instead, our institutions of police, courts, and sometimes schools, do not share information or coordinate in the best interest of the child.

Instead, a new attorney is brought in who knows nothing of Alex's past. The court holds that Lois is only his Child Protection lawyer. She knows Alex and could speak meaningfully to the authorities about him in troublesome instances. Instead, the court appoints some other "never-seen-him-before" attorney to defend him. That's how juveniles end up in prison.

Our communities are overdue for a big discussion around how to deal with troubled youth who are wards of the state. A failure at this stage is too often permanent for the child. American juvenile crime statistics are the highest in the industrialized world. Many American juveniles are tried in adult courts. Once a juvenile enters the adult Criminal Justice System, the data is compellingly negative. Criminal Justice seeks to punish, not rehabilitate. Juveniles in Criminal Justice remain in the system for many years.

It would be simple enough to ensure that a single lawyer, who knew and could speak to the court about the child, could address the court in his behalf. There are many proven programs to help juveniles stay out of prison.

The Morbidity and Mortality Weekly Report from June 25, 2004, (www.cdc.gov/mmwr), has a new study that shows a terrific success rate for juvenile boys (just like Alex). Therapeutic foster care resulting in 73.5 percent fewer felony assaults and a 37 percent reduction in crime after intervention rather than those placed in other kinds of group care. These are the best results I've seen in my years of research.

The study found that for every dollar spent in justice system costs, that same dollar spent on therapeutic foster care saved $14.07. At the rate we are now moving to implement new and better programs, I would estimate ten to twenty years will pass before this one gets the attention it needs to launch nationally (without your involvement).

Alex's sexuality issues are uncomfortable to social workers and there are few policies that help direct workers who must work with children's sexuality issues. Because of this, my friend Alex has not received timely, effective care for what has tortured him most. It is not that the care Alex has received has been cheap or that childcare workers are at fault. The care Alex has received to this point has been very expensive. In his seventh year as a state ward, Alex finally met a counselor who could talk to him about his sexuality issues. The care Alex needed came too little and too late. He had already fallen into experimenting with prostituting himself.

I estimate that Alex has cost the community $30,000 to $50,000 a year for the last eight years, with the very real potential of spending another thirty or forty years in institutions. There are thousands of boys just like him in our communities.

As a middle-class kid who has had only a few bad days that I didn't bring on myself, it is a cosmic incongruity that I should know so many charming children who lead these desperately unhappy lives.

This is not only painful for any caring person to observe, it is also expensive and unproductive for the community to maintain, and it makes for a much more dangerous society as well.

We have a system in which almost all of the children in Juvenile Justice have come out of the Child Protection System and over half of the children in Juvenile Justice have diagnosable mental illness, (Children's Defense Fund, 2001).

These truths should drive our institutional policies; yet, they are not even known to the average politician or educational administrator.

The Juvenile Justice System has become the dumping ground for abused children with mental health problems. Our state and federal policies are setting these children up for a life of failure and incarceration and causing us to live in fear of our own safety.

We, as citizens, are all accomplices in this abomination. We can do better.

Call to Action

It doesn't take much to discover a story like Alex's.

You might read about children like him, you might hear about children like him, you might experience children like him.

Make it your business to find out how your community handles very troubled children.

Learn about your county's Child Protection System and do some small thing to make a difference in a troubled child's life.

Investigate mentoring programs in your community.

Investigate your county's Child Protection System.

Investigate mental health resources for children in your community:

National Institute of Mental health:
nimh.nih.gov/healthinformation/childmenu

Child Welfare League of America: **cwla.org**

A Home Within: **ahomewithin.org**

American Academy of Child and
Adolescent Psychiatry: **ascap.org**

American Academy of Pediatrics: **aap.org**

Comprehensive Mental Health Services Program for Children
and their Families: **Mentalhealth.samhsa.gov/cmhs**

National Child Welfare Resource Center for
Family Centered Practice: **cwresource.org**

The Carter Center Mental Health Program:
cartercenter.org/healthprograms/program6.htm

Screening for Mental Health, Inc:
mentalhealthscreening.org

TWO
Nancy
(The Under-Reporting of Abuse)

When you meet a third-grade child for the first time, it is hard to visualize her being sexually abused, beaten, or tortured.

Nancy's case files alluded to possible sex abuse by the mother's live-in lover. Writing about child sex abuse is not easy for most child-care workers. Between the personal discomfort of writing about it, and the difficulty of proving exactly what happened, much child sex abuse is minimized or not reported at all.

You know what you heard and you know what you saw, but it can be very difficult for a social worker to write down the nuances of a child's remembering a trauma, or the events that were significant and who was responsible for what happened.

Much abuse results from the parent leaving the child in the care of abusive relatives or friends. As a culture, we don't like dealing with this topic, and we do many things to euphemize, obfuscate, and avoid it.

Visiting with parents whose children are being taken away from them by the courts is always uncomfortable. My first visit to Nancy's mother was more stressful than usual because she was incoherent from drug abuse, and she had started a fire in her apartment. By overloading a washing machine in the apartment, she had burned out the machine's electric motor and started an electrical fire. This very smoky fire set off the building's smoke alarms, frightening the tenants. This created a giant and unnecessary chaos—simply because she refused to tell anyone where the fire was.

Every cell in my body wanted to inform the residents of this minor stupidity. I decided as an independent observer that my role would have been compromised, had I spoken out. I chose to observe the workings of a crack cocaine mother in her element.

This was a mind-numbing, unbelievably rotten atmosphere in which to bring up a child. Crack cocaine really does "own" the user. There *was* no one home. She could no more defend her children against the sexual advances of her abusive lover than she could quit using crack cocaine.

Her lover was a violent abuser of women and young girls. Age meant nothing to him—six years old was kinda how he liked 'em. When the written case histories include peanut butter on penises as described by seven-year-old girls and brutal beatings repeated by all the siblings, a guardian ad-Litem begins to understand what daily life was like for Nancy and her siblings.

Mother was a serious drug user and often unconscious or in a stupor. She was unable to provide emotional support or keep her sex pervert lover from abusing her children. Each day brought a series of sex acts and beatings for Nancy. The sex and abuse went on for about four years. It was hard for me to tell how much abuse happened directly to the younger children, but they were certainly in the room (and the bed) when their older sister was being abused. The children were unable to turn to anyone for help. Their mother was absolutely controlled by her drug habit and not able to give these children even the most basic feelings of love or security.

In the courtroom, it was easy to tell the judge that this mother was unfit. I had seen real live crack behavior and read enough case histories to firmly believe this was an over-the-top case.

When I first met seven-year-old Nancy at the initial court hearing, a social worker asked me to drive this child to her new group home after court.

I have never been so frightened of a young girl in my life. Nancy had just been removed from her abusive home, where she had been beaten and raped.

Nancy had suffered years of severe and daily mental, physical, and sexual abuse. Her response to any authority figure was hate and fear. She shook all the way to the group home. Her eyes were wide and fearful. She had an extremely limited vocabulary, and I could not understand her speech. She was afraid of me; I was afraid of her.

> **"It is sobering to note that 30-50 percent of children murdered by their parents or caretakers were killed after violence was identified by social service agencies when the children remained at home or were returned home after**

> **short-term placements . . . parents who severely hurt or kill their children are 'categorically different' from parents who have neglected their children without life-threatening harm."**
> (*Turmoil to Turning Points*, **Richard Kagan, p. 198.**)

About 1400 American children a year are murdered by their parents. Nationally, over a million charges of child abuse are brought each year, of which about two-thirds are investigated and one-third result in the child's removal from the home.

Abusive adults often are in violent marriages or relationships. Alcoholism and drug addiction are commonly the platform on which the abusive adult's life is built. Children come in second or third place after the daily scramble for chemical highs that inevitably leave the children in need of food, attention, love, and safety. Violence and abuse is common within the home of addicted and alcoholic adults.

Regular acts of crime, violence, alcohol and drug abuse become woven into the everyday life of children who are neglected, frightened, beaten, and molested until someone from the outside stops it. Some children are lucky enough to be removed at a young age and find the help they need to become normal adults. Others are not.

Often severe child abuse is followed by indifference of the parent. The addicted or alcoholic adult is in a violent relationship with a spouse or lover and simply cannot parent. The child witnesses violent acts and violent language. It is hard to know what impacts a child more, being beaten and abused by a parent, or watching a sibling or parent beaten in a violent alcoholic or drug-crazed assault. The trauma for the child may very well be the same for either act.

Parental drug addiction and violence set the stage for the horrendous acts of physical and sexual abuse against the child. The child has nowhere to turn and no one to talk to, no one to love, and no one to trust. There is no caring adult to help make things better. Instead, this violent home full of addiction and abuse becomes the most cruel and lonesome place on the planet for a child. Growing up in this environment creates the most tortured souls in the universe.

Within a few weeks of the initial hearing, all of Nancy's younger brothers and sisters had been interviewed and the story that unfolded was pornographic and painful to even imagine.

All the children had become "sexualized" once the act was performed with the oldest girl in the communal bed. Crack cocaine is the mother of many sins. Three young children watching the oldest being abused repeatedly brings them all into an early dysfunctional adulthood.

One of the sadder consequences of these circumstances is that traumatized children become unstable and revert to old and terrible behaviors when they see each other. Old behaviors don't evaporate when children are removed from toxic homes.

It was painfully evident that these children could not be adopted together. Children losing their mother could not be placed in the same home with their siblings because their shared history together was so bad. It made them do horrific things, like being sexually active, when they were together. Not that they didn't have sexual issues when they weren't together, only that their behaviors were more manageable.

Siblings love to be (and need to be) reunited, but it made these children crazy. Each child made progress developing new and better coping skills in their new adoptive homes. Being around their brothers and sisters triggered insane behavior reversals that would last for weeks and months after each visit. The new adoptive parents found reunification visits unbearable. It caused everyone great pain and a real sadness to keep these siblings apart. Many years later, they still remain apart.

It's important to understand that behaviors of neglected children are learned—and are only a rational response to their insane circumstances and the pain inflicted upon them. I can only guess at the isolation and abandonment felt by these youngsters. I can see the acting out, rejection, and hopelessness they respond to their environment with. All the children I have come to know want to be calm, smart, friendly, and normal. They simply don't know how.

Child abuse is terrible in both its emotional and physical consequences. Studies show that the brain of a severely abused child is altered in how it processes information. What a child concentrates on, how he/she identifies danger, become paramount. Attention is focused on danger and avoidance of danger. This precludes normal learning patterns. Regular brain development and learning patterns are replaced by neurotic responses to violence and trauma.

Adult women who have been raped see their world in a frightening new way after the rape. They become much more aware of the danger that surrounds them. Out of fear, people who have been terribly assaulted change their old routes and old habits. A whole lifetime of behaviors becomes forgotten. Safety first.

Abused children are fully aware of where the next danger will come from. Their perception and attention are welded to where the next trauma might be. Normal children have the luxury to concentrate on learning, playing, or making friends. Invisible Children are always busy protecting themselves.

Abused and neglected children are "hyper-vigilant" all the time. They have become neurological attuned to their own dangerous world. Hyper-vigilant children are unable to concentrate and they often don't possess the skills for learning in school, making friends, or normal play.

> **"Approximately 300,000 children are recognized (by public officials such as those in protective service and mental health agencies and the schools) as being sexually abused."** *(Violence Against Children in the Family and the Community,* **edited by Penelope K. Trickett & Cynthia J. Schellenbach, American Psychological Association, Washington, DC, p. 60.)**

In my experience, with a progressive court system and its handling of child sexual abuse, I am firmly convinced that child sexual abuse is both under-reported and under-addressed in the best systems. Other court systems, without reporting requirements and established methods of reporting, make it impossible to have an accurate idea of the magnitude of the problem in a community. Many communities just don't know.

I have yet to see a child taken from a family that wasn't an extreme example of repeated serious abuse and maltreatment. Not that it can't or doesn't happen. Well-trained social service workers don't have time to deal with the less serious cases of child abuse. Social workers are too busy with real neglect and abuse cases to make those kinds of mistakes. If there is a problem, it most likely has to do with funding and training of the people in the field.

Blaming social workers for children falling through the cracks of a system is almost always just plain scapegoating to avoid the real issue of poor policy making. Social workers need the public's support and resources, not scorn, second-rate training, and low wages. Their work is difficult, and it takes great energy and commitment. The least we can do is to see that they are supported in their efforts.

Humans are complex psychological beings. Children grieve the loss of their parents, even abusive parents. It is not rare that even terribly abused children want to stay with their abusive parents. These are deep-rooted emotions of bonding and attachment that are not easily explained or dealt with.

Children who lose their parents and their siblings experience profound grief. The grief they experience is severe and lasts a very long time. I have had abandoned children tell me how impossible it is to understand what has happened to them and how hard it is to sort out the question of "why." Timely, professional therapy can be helpful. Getting children to simply feel "normal" can save a great deal of human suffering and expense to the state.

The children I have worked with have not received enough timely, professional therapy.

Our communities seem to think we are saving money by not making mental health services available on a large scale and in a timely fashion to abused and neglected children.

Nancy hates herself as much as anyone I have ever known. Abused children believe they are responsible for what has happened to them. They feel like unworthy beings. I have watched Nancy again and again and again refuse the kindness of potential foster and adoptive parents who really loved her and wanted so much to help her find herself.

Isn't it sad that her long-time sexual perpetrator gets to remain in the home, sleeping in the same bed, while she and her siblings were cast out into the frightening cold world of County Child Protection? Residential treatment centers, sexual acting-out, attempts at suicide, and not fitting into school, indicate the great need Invisible Children have to make it to *normal.*

Fortunate abandoned children find adoptive homes. The less fortunate can live for many years moving from placement to placement, with no friends, poor achievement in all areas of endeavor, and no long-term adults in their lives. They are alone in this world. They don't even have themselves as friends.

Older children and troubled children are not as attractive as younger children are. They are much more work to have in the home. They are not as likely to be adopted as the younger, less-troubled children are. The feeling of worthlessness and rejection is a very real state that needs much more awareness building and attention by all our Child Protection Systems.

This is not meant to reflect on the efforts of workers in the system. They are not therapists or policy makers. Without being directed by enlightened public policy, workers can only work within the limits of the policies that exist. Sorting out policy objectives and programs that will reach these goals are legislative endeavors that will be decided by voters.

Self-loathing is totally self-induced and addressable. If not addressed, self-hate perpetuates itself and presents a moment-to-moment barrier to a child's development. As I write this book, there are about fifty child psychiatrists in the state of Minnesota. Not nearly enough to properly address the issues that need to be confronted by the state's abused and neglected children.

It is not within the scope of this book to research each state in each area of comparison. I do know that there are states with less attention to the mental health issues of children. New Jersey recently cut funding for all mental health services within its statewide school system.

Think about it. Nancy was molested, beaten, and psychologically tortured for many years. Her perpetrator was never charged with the crimes he committed against her and her siblings. He committed daily acts of sexual abuse and regularly beating a very young girl and probably her younger siblings.

Victims, especially child victims of this kind of abuse, blame themselves. This is truly a humiliated, tortured, and abandoned child, with all the attendant mental health issues. I expect the depths of her disturbances will be with her forever. She "knows" no one wants her and she is not mentally stable enough to allow caring people to help her. We could mitigate the damages of this worst-case scenario in several ways:

- Throw out the Imminent Harm doctrine. Most other industrialized nations don't allow children to remain in the homes of abusive parents. In America, we don't remove children from a home unless they are bruised or bleeding. Parents whose lives are controlled by certain drugs (crack cocaine, heroin, and methamphetamine are three that come to mind) are, by definition, guaranteed to satisfy their drug habits at the direct expense of their child. Drug addicts can't take care of themselves, let alone adequately provide for a child. Many drug user homes have no food. Many drug user homes have guns, dangerous chemicals, and prostitution. The toxic, illegal, and dangerous environment of meth labs, guns, and violence, are, by definition, dangerous to the well-being of a child.

Five-year-olds are prostituted and get high with the help of their addicted parents. What kind of a life would you expect this child to have? It is our collective responsibility to care enough about children to adopt legislation and programs that, at the very least, create systems and policies for dealing with the most dangerous and problematic of these conditions. Not to do so makes us a party to a child's future life of crime, poverty, violence, and early pregnancy that has come to define our nation. Consider these ideas:

- Provide immediate and long-term mental health services to children with Nancy's profile.

- Don't let an abandoned child drift for years within a system, be treated by a multitude of people, and live in multiple foster homes. Make a concerted effort to see that worst-case children get best-case treatment with consistency in treatment and providers in their lives.

- For the children who do linger two years or longer as state wards, when they turn eighteen we must not cast them loose and expect them to function as normal adults. They are immature and often bound for prison or early pregnancy. No one wins if that happens. We need extended care and concern for these troubled young people. They simply do not have the tools to cope with society. Make sure your community is providing services to this group of children. Parenting classes, mental health services, after-school programs, and child-friendly legislation provide the path to stable and capable youth.

Nancy was placed on long-lasting birth control at age eleven by a judge. Her learned behaviors are not going to disappear because she has been moved from an abusive home. Nancy stole out of her group home placement her first week and seduced a man at a local bar. By age fourteen, she had multiple sexual contacts, some with pimps. She is not able to prosecute her current molester because she does not have the confidence to do so.

Long after the court removed the children from the toxic home, Nancy's perpetrator was still visiting Nancy's mother and using crack cocaine. From what I have seen, the man who initially abused Nancy and her siblings never changed his lifestyle or lost anything because of his criminal behaviors.

As the guardian ad-Litem who came to observe Nancy and her brothers and sisters in their transition through the court system, I see the sadness and unfairness of an adult-centered institution. Nancy and her brothers and sister felt humiliated scrutinized and punished by an adult-centered and underfunded Child Protection System. This is in addition to the crimes that were committed against them. These children will carry the effects of his abuses to the ends of their lives.

Nancy's abuser also beat and abused Nancy's mother in the children's presence.

"Children living with an abused mother also are at serious risk for sexual abuse; they are twelve to fourteen times more likely to experience sexual abuse by the mother's partner as well as seven times more likely to report sexual abuse occurring outside the home." *(Violence Against Children in the Family and the Community,* **edited by Penelope K. Trickett & Cynthia J. Schellenbach, American Psychological Association, Washington, DC, p. 60.)**

Permanency work is complicated and painful, and it is the true test of discovering if the monsters have been tamed. When a child cannot be adopted because of her own subterfuge, the future is dark indeed. The thing she needs the most is the thing she believes she is not worthy of having.

She needs so badly to be loved, but she cannot allow herself to be loved. With her negative self-image, she is unable to learn or to make friends. She is ridiculed at school. She knows and feels that she is not a normal person. What do you think she sees as her choices?

For five years I have tried to see Nancy regularly. She is now a teenager. We are still pretty good friends. She may or may not know that I am the only person who stayed in her life since she was removed from her birth home. She has the vocabulary and educational standing of a nine-year-old. She wants a baby. She has never experienced love in her life, and she knows a baby would make her feel love. She knows she would love the baby.

Many girls like Nancy have an extremely poor grasp of reality and a profound drive to have a baby. She will do almost anything to be accepted by some dysfunctional male figure. Very little exists in her life outside of being driven by destructive, neurotic compulsions.

Nancy has no trusted friends, nor does she trust any adult or authority figure. She listens to nobody and lives in a twisted world of false hopes and false assumptions. She gravitates toward the wrong people, and avoids (like crazy) those people who might be honest and helpful. Nancy does this because she does not feel *worthy*. She has told me so, and she has proved it at least one hundred times.

I fully expect Nancy will have her baby(ies). I don't believe she has, or will, develop the skills to raise a child, or find a kind and loving man to be the father. The rest of her life looks like it might be as painful as her past. Her tortured first seven years were too traumatic to be counseled away by the semi-serious approach to mental health—one more of her bad fortunes.

At times abused children seem to be adjusting well to their new surroundings. I think it is often simply another learned behavior to get by in another uncomfortable situation. That is, the old behavior has not been unlearned or cast out. The new behavior is a mask that works in a current situation.

Old behaviors must be dealt with, understood, and managed for abandoned children to meld back into society. I don't think current public policy deals with this awful truth. Our standards for success in dealing with abused and neglected children are too low. Small achievements seem to warrant a stamp of success. Too soon the state decides: that's enough of the state's resources for that one.

Our communities sometimes act as if they have accomplished their responsibility by removing children from toxic environments. These children need more. Invisible Children deserve to have the coping skills and abilities to receive an education, make friends, and lead a fulfilling life.

The toxins of abuse are embedded deeply within the child. The child needs to be made well and have their toxins dealt with. The state, as the child's new parent, must appreciate what the child needs to avoid self-destruction and move towards normalcy. To ignore this is to allow the child to fight with his demons without the help necessary to win the battle.

Even the kindest foster and adoptive parents will fail if they don't understand the workings of the mind and best practices for mental health issues. This is too much to ask of untrained parents.

This perfectly beautiful young girl slipped from being an abused child to being an abandoned child (as a state ward), and she missed the potential for treatment or being part of a loving family. There is a very good chance that soon she will be another pregnant and misguided adult functioning poorly on the streets.

How is she to pass on a realistic perspective of family and social life to her children if she has no idea herself?

UNICEF found that the teen pregnancy rate in America is twice that of the industrialized nations. For every one thousand American women, fifteen to nineteen, there were 52.1 births compared to 2.9 in Korea and 4.6 in Japan. About 22 percent of American twenty-year-olds had a child in their teens.

> **"The high incidence of births to teen mothers contributes to our hostile environment. A widely accepted conclusion is that children**

having babies is not a good idea, for the mother firstly, and certainly not for the baby. Many advocacy organizations in America have recognized this and the result of their efforts has been a decline in teen births to the lowest level in sixty years. That is the good news. The bad news is that this is still the highest rate of teen births among America's peer nations… Magnifying this disturbing picture is that American teen abortions rank nearly ten times higher than the European Union experience. In fact, only Russia has a higher teen abortion rate and Bulgaria, Belarus, Estonia, Hungary, and Latvia have rates most similar to those in the U.S." (David Strand, *Nation Out of Step*, pp. 31–32.)

Almost one-half of all pregnancies in America are unintended. Unintended pregnancy is medically costly in terms of the precluded opportunity for preconception care and counseling. Youth pregnancy also means an increased likelihood of late or no prenatal care, increased risk for low birth-weight, and increased risk for infant mortality.

A study in Rochester, New York, found that the risk of becoming pregnant is approximately 50 percent higher among high school girls who experience maltreatment during their childhood. Approximately half of these girls experienced more than one form of maltreatment, including sexual abuse.

Girls are sexually abused about three times more often than boys are. Current statistics put it as one in every three to four girls will be abused before she is eighteen years old. A significant number of children under five are sexually abused each year.

> **"Based on the scientific evidence, we face a serious public health challenge regarding sexual health of our nation. Doing nothing is unacceptable. More than anyone, it is our children who will suffer the consequences of our failure to meet these responsibilities." (The Surgeon General's Call to Action to Promote Sexual Health and Responsible Sexual Behavior, July 9, 2001.)**

It is common for children like Nancy to be punished—and not the perpetrator. Her abuser was not involved in the court case. The perpetrator was not her parent, and he was not considered a legal party in the case. He was never charged with any crime or punished in any way for years of molesting children. Did he also abuse other young girls? Is he still abusing young girls?

Nancy and her two brothers and sister will spend the rest of their lives adjusting their behaviors and rationalizing their childhood. Nothing has been easy for any of them. The optimist in me believes Nancy's siblings will be able to deal with life and experience a normal amount of happiness. Nancy will probably not have a normal life. She is living a life of continued sexual abuse, self-abuse, and self-hate.

When counseling comes late, or as a half measure, it is ineffective and less likely to be useful. Counseling that doesn't continue into maturity is ineffective. When counseling is done early and fully, there is a much greater chance the child will maintain a relationship with a counselor and work on those issues for longer and to greater effect.

If I sexually molest a child, I will almost certainly be sent to prison for a long time, unless the victim is my own child. In Nancy's case, had anyone outside her household done these things to her, the state could put him in prison. Children are still chattels and unless a parent kills them, a care-giving perpetrator is not likely to suffer any consequences, outside of losing custody.

Seven years later, I visited Nancy's mother after having been involved in removing her children in three separate court battles. I found she had righted her life. She was struggling to do her best to rebuild a family and live a normal life. In her defense, she had grown up in the same drug-crazed and abusive atmosphere that she had inflicted upon her daughter. I am respectful of her efforts and believe she can make it. She has even called me to let me know that she was trying to buy a house with her new husband.

Most of the little girls I have come to know in the Child Protection System desperately seek the experience of love in their lives. Their own lives have been cold and cruel.

Not having love in one's life leaves a constant and powerful yearning for abused and neglected children.

All of us can understand the loneliness experienced by abandoned children. Some of us can "feel" the pain of a child who has lived without love in their life. We (individually and as a community) can behave kinder towards these children and the institutions they reside in, whether it's our schools, detention centers, jails, or on the street. These children are absolutely everywhere today. Look around you.

The skills of civilization do not just show up.

They are delivered by parents, teachers, and people who care.

Advocate for aggressive and accurate reporting of what occurs in your communities concerning children's issues. Sexual abuse in under-reported in all communities. The problems cannot be solved unless they are identified.

Immediate and adequate mental health therapies are absolutely critical to saving the lives of children in Nancy's condition. Raped for years in a cold violent home, she needed extensive professional help once she was removed from her home. It was not available, and she will suffer forever because of this. Does your community offer acceptable mental health services for brutally assaulted children? Draw attention to the importance of adequate mental health services for abused and neglected children in your community.

Women who live in homeless shelters report assaults eleven times more often than abused women do elsewhere. Assaults on women forced to live in homeless shelters are also more serious and their children are also much more vulnerable to the violence and sex abuse that accompanies these assaults.

Call to Action

Find out what you can do to support people in your community who are forced to live in shelters. What are the conditions within homeless and women's shelters in your neighborhood? Are children at risk? Help to end the violence of abused women and children.

www.endabuse.org
(Family violence research)

www.savethechildren.org
(Child poverty)

www.ACLU.org
(American Civil Liberties Union,
defending civil rights)

www.bwss.org
(Battered Women Support Services)

www.bwjp.org
(Battered Women Justice Program)

THREE

The Doctrine of Imminent Harm

(A Law that Hurts Children)

Federal law dictates state law. Counties must follow both state and federal law for their laws to be valid or enforceable.

The Doctrine of Imminent Harm is a federal law that holds that a child is not to be removed from a parent unless the child is in imminent harm. As I have seen it translated, children are to remain in the home unless they are bruised or bleeding. Children can be pretty badly beaten without obvious signs of trauma. Countless children are molested without being discovered by authorities. Many communities are struggling to have their police and courts systems deal effectively with abused children.

Two sisters, Ann, age five, and Sharon, age seven, lived with a crack cocaine-using mother. Police had been called to their home forty-nine times over three years. The juvenile officer confessed to me that she had heard the mother, on several occasions, hatefully tell Sharon (her daughter) that she wished Sharon were dead and that she (the child) had never been born.

Multiple police reports were made of gunfire, drug use, and prostitution at the home. A known prostitute lived with the now fatherless family. The seven-year-old had been sexually abused. I believe that she had also been prostituted.

Many opportunities existed to take these poor abused girls from their abusive mother, but the Doctrine of Imminent Harm forbade police to remove the children. For three years the police were aware of the bizarre happenings within this home, yet they left these girls to be hated and tortured by their mother. This was an educated and suburban, twenty-first century police force.

Imminent Harm allows a variety of evils to be heaped on trapped children. It keeps children living within tragic circumstances with no accountability of the parent or the county. If laws are ever going to protect children, the Doctrine of Imminent Harm will need to include the psychological damage so obviously perpetrated upon these girls. Then the police might have taken the tortured children out of the home on the first or second police call to the home with far better chances for the children's recovery.

Three years of daily exposure to drugs, violence, and sexual abuse creates patterns of behaviors that will not be easily counseled away.

A percentage of experienced police officers become jaded by their continual exposure to children of drug users, violence, and criminals. Some officers don't go out of their way to bring attention to the plight of the children they know are suffering. Policing is a complex business that demands many skills to be an effective officer.

Domestic issues are not at the top of the list of the police officers that I have come to know. Most police officers would rather not be put in the role of policing families. The dynamics of enforcing laws against fathers and mothers concerning the condition and treatment of their children requires a level of understanding and training that not many police officers receive.

Police friends have shared their stories about being unable to withhold their laughter, as an eleven-year-old girl told them about her sexual abuse in the home. It was, in fact, a horrific story. These officers simply didn't have empathy for her family life. They did not view her as credible or human enough to take her seriously. I can only assume that after seeing hundreds of mentally ill and abused children in toxic homes, some officers become insensitive. It's certainly not an ideal situation for children to be seeking justice.

The only reason Ann and Sharon were finally removed from this home was that during the forty-ninth police call to the home, the older girl tried to kill the younger one by jumping on her neck. Children who have been terribly abused often do terrible things to other people. Mother lost custody of her children. No one in her family supported her keeping custody.

I do not believe the sexual abuse issues in this case were ever fully recognized or addressed. I am also convinced child sex abuse is grossly under-reported in the best Child Protection Systems.

- Minnesota reported 897 child sexual abuse cases in 2002. If that's true, I knew of about forty of them; and I was only one of about three hundred guardian ad-Litems that year. I don't believe Minnesota children experienced only 897 cases of child sex abuse in 2002.

Abused and neglected children rightfully fear authority. The most important (adult) authority figure in their life beat, molested, or neglected them to the extent that the state removed them from their own home for their own safety. I suspect that less than one out of ten abused children who have been through the Child Protection System would ever voluntarily spill their guts to a police officer or any unfamiliar well meaning teacher or other (adult) authority figure.

How does a frightened seven-year-old child, who has been living in fear in the painful insane world of drugs and sexual abuse for three or four years, even begin to attend to her studies in a classroom? Anxiety and fear consume children who have been abused. They have little or no attention for the subject matter. She is a very needy child, who is not able to relax, do her work, enjoy her friends or the school experience.

Trust will always be an issue. I've seen it go on far into adulthood. Trust issues last forever. Many of these children will never have a significant other. They simply can't allow people that close to them; the pain of loss and lack of trust is too great. This becomes a very real mental awareness that evolves from not being able to trust the most important adult in her life.

For children who are severely abused over long periods, trust issues and extreme behaviors learned for self-protection become rock hard, constant, and detrimental to living normally in our society. Their abnormal behaviors brand them as *different*. Their difficult behaviors result in their being treated poorly by teachers, authority figures, and peers.

Children in school are rough on each other. Adults don't care why Invisible Children don't follow orders or behave so poorly. There are simply consequences. Without adequate counseling and treatment, these children will continue to disappoint us in school and in the community and receive the consequences of prison and pregnancy.

Children who have been seriously abused act out in painful ways. They become a bundle of explosive behaviors. Invisible Children stab people, light fires, and hurt themselves and those around them. Starved children cut open furniture and hide food. Love-starved, neglected, and abandoned children have a giant hole in them that can't be filled. Abused children do terrible things in order to try to fill that hole.

Invisible Children desperately want and need love, but they do things that ensure they will never receive love. Abused and neglected children can't trust enough to have love. They often can't be taught to trust authority or anyone else, and sometimes this is forever. Imagine going through life without ever being able to trust another person. Children, who have lost their mother through neglect and abuse often are unable to relearn how to trust or how to love.

Children believe they are responsible for the bad things that have happened to them. Abused and neglected children can hate themselves with a persistent self-loathing that hurts to observe, isn't easily described, and doesn't lend itself well to therapy. Molested children feel cheap and dirty. Molested boys have the additional stigma of homosexuality and loss of manhood issues. I know a sixty-five-year-old professional man who, after fifty years of therapy, still fights the demons from the things that happened to him in his childhood.

- Twenty percent of American Indian ninth grade girls and 17 percent of Chicano/Latino ninth grade girls tried to kill themselves during the 1995 school year.

- About 8 percent of the African American, Asian, and white student population attempted suicide that year also. (*Getting it All Together; the Health and Well Being of Minnesota Youth.*)

Medicating children without ample monitoring of the results is wrong, and it occurs all too often. There is no question that meds keep some children from hurting themselves, their peers, and authority figures. Meds without sufficient therapy are a questionable benefit in the long term. These are complex issues, and I wish to stress the need for more dialogue and better answers.

Drugs for attention deficit and other behavior modifying drugs have become a greater cost to Americans than for antibiotics and asthma drugs. The legal medicating of young Americans without adequate mental health services is a cultural and statistical phenomenon that needs attention.

While immediate dangerous behaviors may be controlled through successful drug regimens, long-term coping skills and mental health programs will more likely create meaningful change within the child. It is all too common for adolescents to quit their legal drug program and begin to medicate themselves in other ways (illegal drugs and alcohol).

Once the child quits the drug program, unmanageable behaviors return and life becomes troublesome for the child and the community. It's hard to overstate the outrageous and dangerous behaviors these children exhibit when they are not being treated for their mental health problems. Our high crime and incarceration rates are a growing reflection of our inadequate solution to this problem. It is only learned coping skills and behavior modification that will keep children out of the Criminal Justice System, not medications without therapy.

Abandoned children respond well to art, music, dance, and theatre. Mentors and sincere adults can also have a big impact on the development of an abused child. Someone or something needs to fill the void. School, marginal attempts at therapy, and all the efforts of well-intentioned people have made almost no impact on the long-term improvement of children I have worked with. Consistent and long term mental health programs work best to heal damaged children.

According to the U.S. Department of State, America has spent *four trillion dollars* on its military since the end of the cold war. Voters are steadfastly behind the spending of security dollars. Strong arguments can be made that these military dollars have served to create a less secure and more hostile world, rather than a safer, better-educated, and smarter world.

Our communities complain about the spending of tax money for schools and programs that could help educate and uplift our community. If we were to build more schools and wage less war, we would have safer cities and a much smaller population of troubled citizens.

In many communities there is a great shortfall of support for mental health services for abused and abandoned children.

Too many communities use medication instead of education and therapy to behavior problems of troubled children.

Dollars invested in mental health services and early childhood programs have proven to be far and away the best investments a society can make (see chapter 5).

Call to Action

Mental health issues are under-addressed in our communities. While there may not be simple solutions to the complex problems of children with mental illness, it is obvious their needs are not being addressed adequately today. It should be clear that Prozac without therapy is wrong and that early mental health therapy will have far better results than waiting until the symptoms explode into dangerous behavior.

Become a proponent of mental health services for children. As you become more aware of the chasm that exists between what is available and what is necessary, you will find it easy to lobby for change. The insurance industry and politicians have stonewalled this issue for many years. It's of primary concern for Invisible Children, and it wouldn't hurt the rest of us to have more access to mental health services either.

Insurance companies fear the added costs and have a giant lobby to persuade our political leaders that change is not needed. Let your political leaders know you expect them to provide mental health services in your schools and for abused and neglected children. Regularly provide your local governing officials information on the need for more mental health services within your schools, Child Protection, and Juvenile Justice System.

Lobbying is big business (in 2001, $1.55 billion). There are about 67,000 lobbyists calling on American lawmakers. Abused and neglected children can't call their legislators, nor can they hire a lobbyist. It's up to concerned citizens to lobby for laws that affect the quality of the lives of neglected children.

Email, write, and call your lawmakers:

www.house.gov
(U.S. House of Representatives)

www.senate.gov
(U.S. Senate)

FOUR
Who Are We Protecting?
(Criminals or Children?)

My first three guardian ad-Litem cases involved long discussions with parole officers and police officers who had been dealing with the parents of the children I was appointed guardian for. It occurred to me that the children were barely considered relevant by any of the officers I spoke to. I was given the distinct feeling that it was the rights of the adults that were being protected without much thought given to abused or neglected children.

In the case of the forty-nine police calls to the home of the two young girls described earlier, the juvenile officer did not think it her business on forty-eight of those calls to remove those children from the home. Unless a child's life was in immediate danger, the officers were not concerned with protecting them.

Police work within the laws that are written for them to enforce. I cannot blame the police for leaving children in terrifying and toxic environments. It's not the fault of the police that our laws do not protect children. It is the jurisdiction of a society and the lawmakers to make laws that will take children out of terrifying and toxic environments. It is the responsibility of the citizenry to make laws that protect children from rape, drug abuse, violence, and insanity.

Police work has become a complex and social business. Law enforcement needs to encompass the protection of children as well as the protection of adults. Eighty years ago, women were chattel and could be legally treated like any other owned object (dogs, cattle, or furniture). Today, the voting public has decided that the rights of children are the same as the rights of women of eighty years ago (chattel). Laws need changing to protect the rights of children.

Child abuse is a criminal act and a police matter. The sooner police are allowed to protect children to the fullest extent of the law, the sooner abused and neglected children can be removed from toxic environments. The repetitious abuse of children can only be short circuited by better reporting and response to obvious signs of child abuse. This speeds the process of repatriating abused children to their own mended families, or finding them loving homes and the therapeutic services they need to be repaired to become normal functioning children.

Currently, parental child abusers don't go to jail unless they have murdered their child. In over eight years, I have seen no arrests for repeated and violent acts against children. Court prerogatives strongly favor adults and children pay the price.

We need better laws that give police clear jurisdiction to act decisively. This would protect children and give courts a clearer mandate for their role in Child Protection. Better legislation would help to take child workers out of the role of criminal investigators and let them concentrate on the healing that needs to happen.

Abuse and neglect are statistically significant factors in almost all studies related to adolescent problems—drugs, prostitution, running away, violence, relationship failure, and school performance.

Twice in my career as a guardian, an abusive parent has requested return of custody of his abused child. Once, the court returned the child without checking court documents that forbade reunification (Alex). The second time, within days of being charged with molesting his two-year-old and thirteen-year-old daughters, the abusive father, through a court appointed attorney, filed a motion to return the abused children to the father.

This may appear to be absurd if you are not involved in the case or are unfamiliar with the workings of Child Protection. However, it appears much more ominous to the mother and the children involved. Why would any system allow a stepfather to further threaten his already traumatized stepdaughter, or the mother who protects her child from her ex-husband's criminal and deviant behavior?

The disruption in this family's life was total. Mom and her children left their home and moved a thousand miles away out of fear. That this child molester could hire a lawyer to drag his abused stepdaughters back into his custody was enough to keep the mother and her children awake at night (and very nervous during the day).

An effective working system would show compassion for those who have been traumatized by child rape and other severe abuses. A working system would not needlessly frighten already damaged children. The mother in this case was required to drive back a thousand miles (on multiple occasions) to where the stepfather lived to file charges and engage in the court battle to keep the stepfather from regaining custody of his step-daughters. Both the mother and the teen-aged victim were terrified the system would fail them.

Nationally, Criminal Justice Systems and Family Court Systems need to be encouraged to work together to create barriers to the unfair and frightening fact that *child molesters do have their molested children returned to them.*

These stressful and uncertain proceedings affected the daughter's performance in school and the mother's ability to parent. Parental rights allow parent perpetrators to continue bringing pain and disruption into a child's life long after they have assaulted the child. I have come to know children who have been terribly assaulted by their parents and who live in fear that the county will send them back to live with their abuser because he/she has parental rights. The trauma of rape and brutal abuse is cruel punishment enough for these children. There is no defensible argument for returning abused children to their abusers.

Is it fair to protect the rights of adults at the expense of their children? If not now, when will children deserve their turn at being protected in our society? Should we be studying what the rest of the industrialized world does about caring for, protecting, and educating their children? If you look, you will see that children are protected, cared for, and educated better in the rest of the industrialized world.

Call to Action

Does your community protect children from being returned by the courts to child abusers?

Make a phone call to your community's child court system and ask how children are protected from parents who are known child abusers.

www.pcamn.org
(Prevent Child Abuse Minnesota)

www.preventchildabuse.org
(Prevent Child Abuse U.S.)

FIVE

Return on Investment

(Saving Children and Saving Money)

Many studies have been done indicating the value of investment in early childhood learning. The following pages are an overview of several important studies reviewed by Art Rolnick in the March 2003, *Fedgazette*:

> **"Perry School participants were less likely to be placed in a special education program and had a significantly higher average achievement score at age fourteen than nonparticipants. Over 65 percent of program participants graduated from regular high school compared with 45 percent of nonparticipants. At age twenty-seven, four times as many program participants as nonparticipants earned $2,000 or more per month. And only one-fifth as many program participants as**

nonparticipants were arrested five or more times by age twenty-seven . . .

"The Syracuse Preschool Program provided support for disadvantaged children from prenatal care through age five. Ten years later problems with probation *and criminal offenses were 70 percent less among participants* compared with a control group . . .

"Abecedarian Project in North Carolina, which provided children from low-income families a full-time, high-quality educational experience from infancy through age five, academic achievement in both reading and math was higher for program participants relative to nonparticipants into young adulthood. Furthermore, participants had fewer incidences of grade retention and special education placements by age fifteen.

"The High/Scope study conducted a benefit-cost analysis by converting the benefits and costs found in the study into monetary values in constant 1992 dollars discounted annually at 3 percent. *The researchers found that for every dollar invested in the program during the early 1960s, over $8 in benefits were returned* to the program participants and society as a whole . . .

"We estimate the real internal rate of return for the Perry School program at 16 percent.

"'Real' indicates that the rate of return is adjusted for inflation . . .

"This analysis suggests that early childhood development is underfunded; otherwise, the internal rate of return on an ECDP would be comparable to other public investments . . .

"On the other hand, the High/Scope study may understate the results we could achieve today. First, the High/Scope study doesn't measure positive effects on children born to participant families after the study period. The knowledge gained by parents participating in the program likely transferred to their younger children . . .

"Second, the study may further understate the effects because it doesn't take into account effects on future generations. With increased education and earnings, participants' children would be less likely to commit crime and more likely to achieve higher levels of education and income than if their parents hadn't attended the Perry School program. A chain of poverty may have been broken . . .

"*The returns to ECDPs are especially high when placed next to other spending by governments made in the name of economic development. Yet ECDP is rarely considered as an economic development measure.*"

Italics (emphasis) are added by author.

Mr. Rolnick goes on to explain that most revenue bonding and public investment strategies return under 7 percent and that if we were to simply recognize the real value of Early Childhood Programs, we would get a better value for our investment. He also points out that even the $8 to $16 cost-to-benefit ratio per dollar spent does not include the incalculable value of breaking the cycle of crime and violence within each of these families.

Once a child leaves the treadmill of crime, drugs, violence, teen pregnancy, and institutionalization, future generations of that child's progeny come with him/her.

This has a very real value, or a very real cost, if not valued.

Call to Action

Look for reports or studies on how much your community spends on early childhood programs. Gain an understanding of the economic arguments for educating and saving children. Watch for budget cuts and let your representatives know that saving money by cutting early childhood programs is a false savings as well as unethical legislative stewardship. Educate the people in your immediate circle of influence about the value of early childhood programs.

SIX

Abused Children Impacting Education

(Supporting Educators)

"Public education does not serve a public. It creates a public. And in creating the right kind of public, the schools contribute toward strengthening the kind of public; the schools contribute toward strengthening the spiritual basis of the American Creed. That is how Thomas Jefferson understood it, Horace Mann understood it, and John Dewey understood it. And in fact there is no other way to understand it." (Neil Postman, *The End of Education*, New York: Knopf, 1995.)

Neglect causes chronic problems that interfere with learning and adjusting to social situations. For abused children, school becomes more of an exercise in adapting to others as an outsider does and avoiding more punishment from adults than an exercise in learning. Maladapted children fight, scream, swear, and are often a danger to themselves and the people around them—a very real danger.

- Violence in and around schools is a significant problem. "28 percent of teachers felt that physical conflict among students was a serious-to-moderate problem… 32 percent of teachers felt unsafe in their schools after hours." (Hoffman, *Schools Violence and Society*, Westport, Conn: Praeger, p. 225.)

- Twenty percent of Chicano/Latino ninth graders had been threatened or injured with a weapon on school property compared to 7 percent of white ninth graders.

- On average, 9 percent of Minnesota twelfth graders, and 15 percent of Minnesota ninth graders were threatened or injured with a weapon on school property. ("Getting it All Together: the Health and Well-Being of Minnesota Youth.")

When I attended an inner city high school, violence, drugs, and drop out rates were a fraction of what they are today. The sister high school to the one I graduated from reported a graduation rate of less than 30 percent this year. It also had a number of incidents with weapons. It is a school where teachers regularly fear for their own safety.

Students with a desire to learn have a hard time getting a quality education in this harsh and failing environment. It is not because teachers don't care or are unqualified, but because the behaviors of students with emotional and mental health problems are so disrupting and dangerous. There are a growing number of unmanageable public schools.

In many communities, school violence is unbearable. Quality teachers and administrators leave troubled systems to find less stressful work. Students are sucked into the world of gangs and violence to belong and to stay safe. Much of what occurs within the classrooms and school hallways is acted out on community streets.

Far too many children have heard shots fired and seen dead and wounded classmates. For almost twenty years, the U.S. has lead all the other industrialized nations in statistical comparisons of murder, crime, per capita rates of incarceration, and prison populations.

Without support from the community, schools struggle to provide only safety and instruction to their pupils. Exceptional students are frustrated because it takes more to challenge them, while most resources and attention go to the squeaky wheels of abused and neglected children. As schools become poorer, there is less and less to attract the average student. Troubled children demand a great deal of teacher time and attention to keep from spinning out of control. Teachers need support to handle abused and neglected children in their classrooms.

I watched a nine-year-old girl seriously hurt a public school teacher who was only trying to stop the girl from hurting herself. After she brutally kicked, bit, and gouged him, he smacked her head on a thick oak railing to save himself. It was terrible.

I don't know what I would have done under the circumstances (you had to be there). What teacher signs on for this duty? How many teachers are aware of the depth of the mental health issues their students bring into the classroom with them?

It is not unusual to hear about teachers spending over half of their time managing one or two very troubled children.

These are the children with mental health issues who need help to grow their skills so they *can* sit through an hour-long math class without exhibiting unmanageable behaviors Comprehensive and long-term programs for troubled youth will go a great deal further than the get-tough policies of incarceration and punishment.

Could we create jobs for some of these children? Open recreation centers? Offer adequate counseling and tutoring programs? More than enough studies have proven we are wasting our money on "boot camps" and incarceration for children and juveniles. Boot camps and incarceration only exacerbate the development of more rage and less skill building.

- From October 2002 to October 2003, 460,000 American high school students dropped out of high school.

- In Minneapolis, Minnesota, 48 percent of African American boys dropped out of school in 2002.

- In America, almost 25 percent of teenagers surveyed admitted to using drugs in the 2002-2003 school year (consistent with past five-year average).

- Twenty-three percent of young African American men graduated from Minneapolis public schools… 129 African American men from Hennepin County were accepted into any college at the University of Minnesota in four years (Gary Cunningham, May 24, 2004 speech, University of St. Thomas Law school).

- Minneapolis public schools reported a four-year graduation rate of 47 percent in 2002. Roosevelt

High School graduated 28 percent of its students (Syl Jones, *Minneapolis Star Tribune*, "Just Think What Powell Could Do for America's Kids," December 8, 2004).

- America ranks 49th in world literacy (*New York Times*, December 12, 2004).

- America ranks 28th in mathematical literacy (*New York Times*, December 12, 2004).

- The lifetime cost of allowing one child to drop out of high school and into a life of crime costs between 1.5 and fifteen million dollars (*Children's Defense Fund*, 2001).

Fifty-three other nations have longer school years than the U.S., which at the time of this writing ranked ninety-one among the world's nations in staff-to-student ratios. What if we replaced juvenile boot camps with learning academies, offering well-funded and enjoyable learning experience at the core of the academy?

David Strand, author of *Nation Out of Step*, captured the harsh realities of our attitudes and values, "I am alarmed by the hostile nature of the environment that we adults have created and now tolerate for our nation's children." David worked in eighteen of the twenty-three advanced democracies and lived in four of them. He points out how America now compares itself with emerging and Third World nations, and how we have come to ignore how we rank against the other 800 million people in developed democracies.

Today we compete with the poverty stricken, repressed regimes of Third World countries as a benchmark for more and more quality of life indicators: mortality, literacy, early childhood education, lifting children out of poverty, and crime.

A leading international indicator for the health and well-being of a nation's children are its schools. American schools have been chronically underfunded for years. The issues of school funding and school performance are becoming the same sort of political football that crime and incarceration have become.

Establishing programs for children after school hours with meaningful activities and supervision could cut crime in this country dramatically. We are a nation of two working parents; many are unable to afford after-school programs for their children.

Unwatched and unwanted children are left to their own designs. Without positive role models, children can find themselves in trouble that lasts a lifetime and costs our communities the peace and tranquility enjoyed by most of the world's other developed nations.

Religious groups, the media, student groups, civic groups, and parents could be organized and involved to bring positive and active involvement into schools at all levels. Many models for successful volunteer strategies exist. Most schools have a hard time managing volunteer activities. Children and school systems will benefit when they learn how to attract, organize, and work with community volunteers for a vast array of proven programs.

There is a growing public anger and frustration aimed at the administrators and teachers of the school systems. There is very little understanding of the complex social issues that contribute to the negative statistics and all-too-human results we read about in the paper.

Criticizing teachers, school administrators, and school funding has become a political vote getter that distracts us from the real issues. We are growing away from valuing better schools and caring about student achievement and towards less support for teachers and schools in general.

The "Leave No Child Behind" mentality is causing even the best teachers and administrators to look and feel like failures. People who dedicate their lives to the noble profession of teaching are being blamed for the failure of public education.

Politicians have little justification for their assault on teachers, schools, and administrators. The promise of money, fame, or power does not attract people to teaching. Teachers teach because they love learning, children, and making a difference. We should be ashamed of the degrading assertions that teachers are shirking their work, or administrators are throwing money away (or, in regressive communities, how immigrants are ruining our schools).

> **"Teachers make less than accountants, architects, doctors, lawyers, engineers, judges, health professionals, auditors, and surveyors. They can earn higher salaries teaching in Berlin, Tokyo, Ottawa, or Amsterdam than in New York or Chicago." (Benjamin R. Barber, *Passion For Democracy*, Princeton, NJ: University Press, 1996.)**

Based on 2000 census data, here are the four lowest paid jobs in Minnesota and their annual wages, as reported in the Minnesota Women's Consortium June 9 *Bulletin*: food preparation, $17,253; food preparation and serving, $17,132; child care, $16,493; and dishwashing, $14,002.

> "The state of Massachusetts discovered that 59 percent of teaching candidates flunked a basic reading and writing test. For math, the failure rate climbed to 63 percent. In our free-market economy, you usually get what you pay for . . . new public school teachers spend an average of six years in their profession before leaving to pursue a different career." (David Strand, *Nation Out of Step*.)

Poor pay, radical federal mandates, impossibly difficult inner-city classrooms, continued underfunding, and negative rhetoric of the press and politicians all make for a much less appealing way to earn a living than it did even twenty years ago. Business continues to attract the talent that once filled our schools. Teachers are leaving their chosen profession and entering business. Can you blame them?

> "If we really valued schooling, we'd pay teachers what we pay stockbrokers; if we valued books, we'd spend a little something on the libraries so that adults could read too; if we valued citizenship, we'd give national service and civic education more than pilot status; if we valued children, we wouldn't let them be abused, manipulated, impoverished, and killed in their beds by gang-war crossfire and stray bullets." (Benjamin R. Barber, *Passion For Democracy*, Princeton, NJ: University Press, 1996.)

As a guardian ad-Litem talking to teachers and school administrators, it appears to me the impact of hundreds of thousands of abused and neglected children on our public schools has been understated.

I have read many case histories as a guardian ad-Litem. Axis II (personality) disorders; Bipolar, Attention Deficit Disorder, ADHD, Developmentally Disabled, Neurosis, Psychosis are common to children who have lived with neglect and abuse.

Most of the children I have worked with took daily drug regimens of Prozac, Ritalin, Amphetamines like Adderall and Dexedrine, and other stimulant drugs. Ritalin is a Schedule II stimulant, similar to amphetamines and cocaine, and has the same dependency profile of cocaine.

Well-monitored and administered drug regimens allow many children to function in society. I have come to appreciate how important these drugs are and how complicated their proper monitoring and administration is. We have come to rely too much on prescriptions and not nearly enough on therapy, human contact, and programs to help abused children manage their compulsive behaviors.

Sweden removed Ritalin (1968) because of widespread abuse. America has a fantastic number of children dependent upon psychotropic medications who are not receiving adequate mental health therapy.

Many troubled and medicated youth are mainstreamed into already overcrowded classrooms, generally with no preparation or specific training given to the teachers who must deal with them. This complicates teachers providing a quality education to the rest of their students.

Severely abused and neglected children have had permanent changes in their brain structure. They have learned an entire complex set of behaviors making them anxiety ridden and fearful in an average classroom situation. Invisible Children can be a terror to the teacher and other students.

Attention Deficit Disorder is compounded by fear of failure, which leads to more tension, which leads to more symptoms, which produces more fear. It is a neurotic cycle we now treat mainly with drugs. Rather than teaching children how to relieve their stress and anxiety, we rely on Class II stimulant drugs.

It's a terrible waste of resources to park disturbed children in classrooms, put them on Class II stimulant drugs, and hope for the best. But at this, America is practiced; it is the norm. There are many teachers with two or three of these troubled children in their classrooms.

Wisconsin's graduation rate for African-American students was 41 percent in 2001 (about half of the rate for white students). Minnesota has similar statistics.

Thousands of neurotic and psychotic children in the public school system appear to be almost invisible to educators, administrators, and the public. We have known for years that 50 to 75 percent of the children in the Juvenile Justice System have diagnosable mental illnesses. These children pass through the public school system and are expected to graduate. Only a small fraction of the children who need mental health services receive them.

Because our institutions wait until a child has shown extreme behaviors before prescribing mental health services, therapy often appears to have poor or sporadic success. Child protection workers know which children need therapy and could make quick and effective use of mental health services that would be effective if this were a policy.

There are fewer than one hundred child psychiatrists in the state of Minnesota. There are about eight hundred students to each school counselor in the state of Minnesota. Many other states have similar ratios. We do not understand or value the effects of hyper-vigilance and other psychological responses to rape, violence, drugs, and insanity have on children.

Statistics for mental illness for children within the Child Protection System are hard to find, but I believe they are similar to the statistics within the Juvenile Justice System (50 to 75 percent have diagnosable mental illness).

Without much attention, American schools have been forced to provide protection and education to thousands of disturbed and troubled children. I say protection, but there may not be an adequate word that denotes the relationship between the teacher and the troubled children we are describing.

Most teachers have limited training to provide mental health services, and they are not good substitutes for professional mental health service providers. Even the best schools rarely provide adequate mental health services for their students. Teachers have few choices besides removal and penalization when working with traumatized children.

Without alternatives like therapy and counseling, all that's left is legally drugging children, punishment, and expulsion. People trained in dealing with abused and traumatized children know that more punishment does not work. It's a vicious cycle. More castigation and humiliation only strengthens a student's resolve to fight back to gain some control over their own life.

Understanding a child's fears and motivations can help dramatically in rehabilitating them back into society. As long as physical correction, embarrassment, and tough measures are used as discipline, abused and neglected children will continue to fail at school—and schools will continue to fail the child and the public. There is no dignity or achievement in this for anybody.

> **"A minimum of 7.5 million (at least 12 percent) of the 63 million children in this country are in need of mental health services for emotional or other problems. Of the 7.5 million, the mental health problems of three million of those children are serious or severe. Some estimates suggest as many as 9.5 million children may be in need of mental health treatment. Two million children receive outpatient mental health treatment each year. The U.S. Office of Technology Assessment estimates that 70 percent to 80 percent of American children in need of treatment may not be receiving it."** (*Statistical Record of Children: Trends in the Well-Being of America's Children and Youth 2001*, p. 435.)

Mental illness and the issues surrounding the treatment of Invisible Children stand out as the most significant challenges facing us today. We must build awareness for our political leaders to positively support mental health issues.

"Thirty-two percent of homeless adults had been told by a doctor or nurse within the previous two years that they have schizophrenia, some other type of delusional disorder, major depression, anti-social personality disorder or post traumatic stress disorder. Twenty-eight percent of the men and 41 percent of the women indicated that they had been physically mistreated as children. (Reported from *Minnesota Statewide Survey of Persons Without Permanent Shelter*, 2001).

A British study showed that "British children living in poverty are three times more likely to suffer mental illness than children from wealthier families are. They are also more likely to die in the first year of life, die from childhood accidents, and they live shorter lives than children from wealthier families." (*End Child Poverty Campaign*, www.ecpc.org.uk, April 2001).

Even though great strides have been made in mental health therapies, our institutions don't provide adequate mental health services for children. Psychotic and neurotic children become mentally ill adults with little or no mental health treatments. Classroom teachers are not made aware of the mental health problems or the drug regimens their students bring with them to class.

The state of New Jersey dropped mental health services to students in the public school system in 2004. Disobedient students are being pushed directly into the Justice System. Fifteen to 20 percent of those students were being passed on to the Criminal Justice System where they are likely to remain.

In 2004, Minnesota had 472 failing schools. Politicians work for more testing, less funding, and more accountability. The public and the media continued to grind down morale and question the performance of educators and schools we used to embrace. We hold teachers responsible for the poor support and condition of the educational institutions we refuse to fully fund. How demoralizing it must be to be a teacher.

In 2004, Minnesota was one of twelve states to lose federal funding under Title One, the largest source of federal funds for elementary and secondary education.

> **"Title One schools in New York City lost $657 million dollars, disabled pupils lost $513 million dollars, and teacher-training programs lost $39 million dollars."(*The Nation,* April 19, 2004.)**

Which means "There was seventeen million dollars less for computers in poor communities and twelve million less for programs that included nurses and counselors . . . New York City has more poor kids, more dropouts, lower graduation rates, lower reading scores, more violence, and larger class sizes than anywhere else." (*The Nation*; April 19, 2004.)

New York State courts have taken over management of the state's schools in 2004, because of massive school failures. Several states are in the process of suing the federal government for failing to provide adequate support to the public schools.

Few of us talk about political footballs, negative public and media attention towards education. Fewer still recognize the impact of inadequate funding or disturbed children on the schools. It's easier to point out failure and blame *those people* than to think through the complex social issues that are involved. Blaming immigrants, teachers, or administrators is unfair and it only serves to cause undeserved pain and distract us from the real issues.

The cry for school vouchers gets louder every year. Not much is said about why teachers are willing to teach in private schools for reduced salaries. Many of those teachers will tell you it is because they love teaching, but do not have the ability to deal with the serious problems of uncontrollable children. These children are automatically guaranteed to be in the classrooms of inner city schools and not in the classrooms of private schools. Many teachers (escapees) have purposely left a public school system for a private school system, exchanging higher paychecks for safety and sanity.

Inner city schools have fewer resources and more troubled and mentally ill children than suburban schools. Suburban schools are filled with the children of educated parents who provide their kids with a pre-school education. Suburban kids have vocabularies four and five times larger than the poorer children within the inner city do. Poor, troubled inner city children with emotional and mental health problems find it much harder to succeed in schools than their bright and capable suburban counter parts.

Behaviors for functioning in school and in public are not delivered to a child by an unknown force at a given age. Children with parents who are unable to help them acquire the skills necessary for getting along have to do with what they have.

Teachers and police try to deal civilly with uncivil children who too soon have their own opportunity to be fathers and mothers. Social workers need better training to identify and speak to the severity of the mental health issues they encounter. All parties need to learn how to speak to and monitor seriously damaged children.

Our systems are not functioning to solve these problems. Many of our institutional policies exacerbate the problems. A lack of resources leads to poorly trained providers and inadequate services. To ignore the inter-relatedness of the issues is to guarantee continued failure. How many teachers, police, administrators, and even social workers, are in over their heads when it comes to effectively dealing with a traumatized abused child?

Would it not be useful for a teacher to know that a quarter of her students were prescribed Prozac? At least she would be able to guess at what caused great mood swings and behavior changes in some of her students.

At a dinner at our home with long-time friends and educators, the subject of who's to blame for failing schools came up. My friends blame immigrants within our schools as a big reason for struggling schools. The big expense for English as Second Language classes and providing services to children "not like us" is stretching their capacity for tolerance.

Immigrants today are like the immigrants our ancestors were. They work hard, learn fast, and meld into society. America has always been a nation of immigrants. Blaming them solves nothing. It only distracts us from what is really destroying us. We are living in a time when the drums of divisive politics have turned us from an open and compassionate community to a fearful and divided society distrustful of immigrants and minorities.

> **"In 1910, the peak year for immigration to Minnesota, 29 percent of the state's population was born outside the country . . . district-wide, less than 4 percent of the population currently hails from another country." (Phil Davies, *Fedgazette*, September, 2004.)**

Where were your great grandparents in 1910?

More troublesome to our troubled school systems than immigrants is the fact that the federal government has not fulfilled its commitment to pay for 40 percent of the cost of special education, which was promised by Congress almost thirty years ago. That failed payment costs the state of Minnesota nearly $250 million annually.

Designing an educational system that addresses the mental health issues of a significant proportion of the youth who are in the classrooms will bring better results than pretending the problem doesn't exist or blaming other factors. Choking off funding and incarcerating children has proven to be an ineffective and costly approach to the problem.

> "The who problem of American education seems to come down to this: in American society, almost everyone identifies intellectual excellence with elitism. This attitude not only guarantees the monopolization of educational advantage by the few, it lowers the quality of elite education itself and threatens to bring about a reign of universal ignorance." (Christopher Lasch, *The Culture of Narcissism* New York: Norton, 1991.)

Families provide the greatest portion of a child's learning experience. Most poor children have at least one parent working full-time and many have both parents working. Limited education and economic hardship make it difficult for poor people to provide their children with what they need to succeed. America now trails most of the industrialized world in the percentage of children living in poverty.

Pre-K (kindergarten) programs are extremely important. The educational advantage that average children have over poor children the day they start kindergarten is huge. In one recent study, the vocabulary of middle-class children was almost five times greater than the vocabulary of poor children. I estimate that the vocabulary of children in the Child Protection System to be significantly less than the vocabulary of the average poor child.

Limited vocabularies combined with emotional and mental health problems ensure that most abused and neglected children are learning impaired in the classroom. When these children start school, they do not have the tools to learn. Beginning their educational careers, these abused and neglected children are far behind their classmates. They need early training to be able to succeed, or they will remain under-performers, dropouts, and a failing part of our state institutions.

Wealthy citizens have removed themselves from what used to be the institutions and services common to us all. Their children go to private and suburban schools. Paying for public services they no longer use doesn't please them. People of means are assured of excellent education, good quality daycare, and adequate personal time with their own children. American voters have made quality education and daycare and the concept of relaxed home time an unaffordable luxury for poor people.

It is not uncommon for people earning six or seven dollars an hour to pay $140 per week for daycare. At eight dollars an hour, take home pay can be below $200 a week. It's impossible to adequately provide for a family on the wages that almost half of American families are earning. No insurance, no day care, inadequate housing, often living in high crime neighborhoods where children are not allowed outside to play have become a big part of our American landscape.

Learning occurs in the framework of home and school. Unemployment and low paying jobs without benefits define a majority of African-American families. It's not that poor people don't work as hard as well off people; it is simply that no amount of effort will bring them the resources needed to raise a healthy family.

If poor families are not supported in their efforts to provide a rich learning environment for their babies, our schools will find Invisible Children failing in the public school environment and graduating into crime and early pregnancy. There are no shortcuts.

We have two choices:

1) Either we take advantage of the less expensive methods available to us as a society to support parents of poor and neglected children in the early years of learning development through high quality early childhood programs, or

2) We will continue to spend many times those amounts failing to change behaviors and deal with the chaos from these students in our public education system and later our courts.

It is important to mention the current draining of talent from the poorer classes and their prevalent graduation into early pregnancy and the Juvenile and Criminal Justice systems. In addition to the cost of institutionalizing so many of our citizens, and the crime and social disturbance that arise from mistreating the problems, there is the cost of lost social capital. Social capital is the value of the individual to society. It could be argued that America has done well because we have invested in our children, and those children have gone on to build a rich and productive nation.

Too many fine young minds and talented children are unable to overcome their childhood and are destined to a life of crime and drugs. Early childhood learning and attention to mental health problems will go a long way towards returning these children to a productive life within their own community.

> **"The difference between that poor kid and a criminal is about eight years"** (John Stanoch, repeating Chief Justice Kathleen Blatz quote, Minnesota Business Partnership.)

Call to Action

Support your community's schools, teachers, immigrants, poor people, and abused children. Stand up for the current group at the bottom of the barrel. Most of us have been championed at one time. We are lucky people. It's our turn to return the favor. We know in our hearts that it is not the immigrants, teachers, or children who are wrecking education. It is near-sighted public policy, poor legislative stewardship, and the lack of our support for programs that actually work.

Pre-school programs are affordable, well run, and common throughout the rest of the industrialized world. Only the U.S. makes early childhood learning and day care unaffordable to poor people.

Providing parenting services, social-service programs, and teaching young mothers the importance of good child rearing will benefit all of us. Baby wins, mother wins, and more productive and healthier children will find it easier to learn when they are of school age.

Well-reared children will more likely graduate from high school, and more likely become contributing members to society. Teaching mothers to cease smoking, drinking, and using drugs before childbirth helps prevent severe physical illness and handicaps, as well as future maltreatment. By linking parents with other health and human services, we can reduce the stresses that create maltreatment.

Become a champion of early childhood development programs. Involve your friends, neighbors, and legislators.

SEVEN
What We Teach Our Children
(Unintended Instruction at School)

What are the unintended lessons children are learning in the corporate branded schools of the twenty-first century? Rod Paige, America's recent Secretary of Education, signed a five million dollar contract with the Coca-Cola Company while in his position of Houston Superintendent of Schools.

We are a consuming public. Conspicuous consumption and brand loyalty are our trademarks as Americans. Shop till you drop. Do these lessons serve our children?

> **"Corporate persuaders drum their products for sandwiches, soft drinks, designer jeans, and sneakers in the schools chaining our children to their brands. They have learned their lessons from the tobacco king-makers who proved that rounding up, corralling, and branding children, reward the winners with**

lifelong loyalty . . . Every fourth child is now obese due to obesity rates doubling in the past decade among young kids and tripling among adolescents. According to Satcher, obesity is the leading cause of type 2 diabetes among kids and is a cause of asthma, another epidemic among our urban children."(David Strand, *Nation Out of Step*, p. 38.)

"Four of every five public schools are in violation of a federal law that limits fat content in school lunches to a maximum of thirty percent of total calories" (Barry Yeoman, "Unhappy Meals," *Mother Jones Magazine*, Jan-Feb 2003, p. 43.)

"Obesity-related conditions cost the US 12 percent of its health budget in the 1990s, some $118 billion dollars, more than double the $47 billion attributable to smoking."(Worldwatch Institute, *Chronic Hunger and Obesity Epidemic Eroding Global Progress*, March 2000.)

"Another casualty for children is the effect of diets high in fats and sugars on dental health. Tooth decay is prevalent in more than half of all children ages six to eight, and in two-thirds of all fifteen-year-old kids. According to Dr. Satcher, food-related disease is a silent epidemic affecting our schoolchildren. Unfortunately, we do not have the dental care system implemented all over northern Europe

(nine counties, 150 million people) where public schools are typically staffed with dentists and dental chairs. In fact, it is normal for the European universal health care approach to include free preventative dental care for all people through the age of eighteen . . . taxpayers foot the bill, but the total cost is far less because more costly corrective care is prevented." (David Strand, *Nation Out Of Step*, p. 40.)

Over eight million Americans have some form of eating disorder. We have built into our educational system the teaching of bad eating habits, which fuels our food-obsessed culture, and leads to sickness and disease.

- Are we so poor a nation that we must allow our children to be sold out to the advanced manipulation of the major manufacturers of pop, candy, jeans, and junk foods within our schools?

- Is the contracting of unhealthy food products and their sale and advertising in our schools a good bargain for our society or our children? Or, by facilitating the significant increase in fats and sugars that are known to increase type 2 diabetes, asthma, obesity, and a multitude of other diseases, have we made a deal with the devil?

- Will it cost us more to treat people for these illnesses than it would have to use wisdom in selecting the policies for foods and advertising in our schools?

"The failure of educators to think critically about the impact of school commercialization on the quality of schools is a terrible ethical laps. It's time for the education establishment to think twice before it sells out its students to the highest bidder."(*The Nation*, June 25, 2001.)

Call to Action

Public schools can impact abused and neglected children more than any other force in their lives. If the schools are well run and well funded, children flourish. Support education in any way you can.

Public schools are the most basic level of government. Administrators are easy to reach. Call a school superintendent and ask what they think the community needs to do to show support. Let them know you support them in their efforts and appreciate the good things they do. Make sure they know what you stand for.

Schools can do so much for life skill building and be a place for kids with troubled home lives to prosper. A wealth of volunteers is waiting to be tapped. Organize. Social momentum is a powerful force. The difference between community malaise and a powerful neighborhood movement can be the efforts of one energized person. Help to be, or find, that person.

EIGHT
Drugs and Children
(Another Type of Insanity)

I know parents who put a World War I gas mask on their five-year-old son and watched him smoke marijuana. Parents conflicted with drug addiction make many bad decisions regarding their children. There are parents and caregivers who have had sex with their own two- and three-year-old children. One of my guardian ad-Litem case families prostituted their six-year-old daughter (drugs were involved).

Five-month-old Janie was the youngest of four children. On a freezing January day, when her mother was out cold from her crack induced stupor, Janie's nine-year-old cousin Sharon set her in the tub to wash some of the crusty four-day-old feces off of her. Sharon turned on the cold and the hot water, half filled the tub, and placed the baby into the water. Janie had been crying all morning, so her screams did not register to the young cousin that perhaps the cold water didn't work and the 161 degree hot water was burning the skin off of this five-month-old baby.

Janie still has terribly disfigured legs ten years later. There was no food in the house and several of the children suffered from lead poisoning. The court removed the children from the home after determining there had been repeated abuse and neglect of the children for many years. The police had been to this house on several occasions and observed the condition of the children. The Doctrine of Imminent Harm forbade them from removing the children from the home.

Leaving a child in the home until they are in imminent harm is a bankrupt social policy. Most other industrialized nations remove children who are endangered by their parents in a timely fashion. The American Doctrine of Imminent Harm guarantees that children will suffer much more serious neglect and abuse before the county can act to save a child.

Two key differences between the rest of the industrialized world and American policy that could alter the results we are getting in our schools, cities, and prisons, are the Doctrine of Imminent Harm and recognizing the importance of mental health services provided in a timely fashion.

Think about your own son being taken from you and raised by a mentally unstable drug-addicted family where he is terribly abused for four years and then returned to you to parent. Clearly, you would not know your own child. Clearly, you would need all the professional support available to help your child unlearn the gross and unbearably painful behaviors he had learned to survive.

How do you unteach learned sexual behaviors? How do you deprogram a small child's drug use and familiarity with violence, sex, and drugs that has become a normal part of each day?

"Increasingly, as police . . . fight against the growing methamphetamine scourge, they find children living in a nightmarish world of bizarre behavior by addicted parents, amid chemicals so toxic that authorities sometimes must hose down terrified children before they can put them in a car and take them to a foster home . . . Authorities tracking meth arrests in Minnesota in recent years say that children have been present in at least 30 percent of the cases, with the figure reaching as high as 50 percent in some years . . . In two cases in Colorado, babies died when their strung-out mothers mistakenly fed them from bottles in which they'd stored liquid meth next to other baby bottles in the refrigerator . . . We are seeing cases of acute hepatitis and acute kidney damage in children coming from these meth-lab homes . . . Chemicals used to make meth have burned children's hands and faces and put them at risk for organ and brain damage, respiratory ailments and other problems . . . Children are at risk of being injured by meth-cooking explosions or by the loaded guns and other weapons often kept by meth users . . . . Children are often neglected for days by parents locked in a cycle of binge and sleep, with sometimes violent mood swings in between." (*Minneapolis Star Tribune*, "Meth's Innocent Victims: Kids," September 22, 2004.)

Does it make sense for states to have a standard set of procedures for helping meth-endangered children? Should children have the right to grow up in a home where meth is not manufactured?

According to Joseph Califano, Jr., parents who abuse drugs and alcohol are three times more likely to physically or sexually assault their children, and children of substance-abusing parents are four times more likely to be victims of neglect. If there is to be any hope of preventing child abuse and preserving the natural family unit, he points out, child welfare workers must be trained to detect substance abuse. (Joseph Califano Jr., *The Least Among Us: The Children of Substance-Abusing Parents*, America Press, April 24, 1999.)

- Young children have no place to hide from drug-abusing parents. Today the average age of abused children of substance-abusing parents is under five.

- There are about four hundred thousand children in foster care every year.

- Five hundred thousand babies are born each year exposed to cocaine and other illicit drugs.

- Over six hundred thousand babies are born to drinking mothers every year—137,000 of them are drinking heavily.

- Fetal Alcohol Syndrome is the number one cause of mental retardation in America.

- Each year over twenty thousand babies are abandoned or taken from substance abusing parents at the hospital.

"All other industrialized nations do more to lift their children out of poverty than the United States" (David Strand, *Nation Out of Step*, p. 47.)

America has more financial resources than any other nation.

The state of California has a greater Gross Domestic Product (GDP) than all but six other nations.

Call to Action

Become aware of the suffering inflicted upon the children of drug addicted people in your community. Find out the birthrate of fetal alcohol births at the hospitals in your community and make it known to the media.

Many models used by other industrialized nations are working to lift children out of poverty to create a level playing field for Invisible Children to play on. Each of us can be part of some church, some socially responsible group, or personally see that some child in our community has the benefit of our effort.

Work to make life better for the children of alcoholics and drug addicts.

NINE
Guns and Children
(A Volatile Topic)

On a farm fifteen miles north of Floodwood, a town of fewer than one hundred people in northern Minnesota, I spent my childhood summers. Hunting and firearms have been a part of my life from the time I was old enough to shoot a gun. I have hunted for almost half a century.

I purchased a thirty-two caliber Colt pistol when I operated the scrap yard. Thinking I needed it for self-defense, I carried it with me every day. There was a great deal of crime and violence in my business and the neighborhood it was in.

I also accumulated a collection of weapons that included a Thompson sub-machine gun. I have been threatened with a gun on one occasion, and I have (almost) used a gun in self-defense on another. This is not meant to recommend my past behaviors, only to point out that guns have played a role in my life. There is no doubt in my mind that possessing and carrying weapons during those years put me (and other harmless people) in more danger than if I had not owned guns.

Over a two-year period in my suburban neighborhood two men were shot dead. One bullet in the head from a high caliber pistol killed each one of them. Each shooting took place in the summer, just after dark, about ten in the evening. Each man was walking his dog. Both men were white and about forty years old. I did not attend the funerals.

For many years after the shootings, my neighborhood lived in fear. I expect many dogs were not walked and many night walks were cancelled. I know I didn't walk at night. My wife never would.

Our society has fostered an atmosphere where walking to your car at night after a movie can be a dangerous thing. Teachers in many city schools are afraid of going to their car after school hours. Recently, my family had foreign exchange students from Mexico live with us. The last young woman was rightly concerned about the dangers of our city streets, a fear she did not feel in her own hometown.

Unsafe streets and blighted neighborhoods are a cost to us all. Caring for indigent mothers and their premature, under-weight, fetal alcohol and crack cocaine positive babies is an enormous cost to this nation that could be substantially reduced through better legislative stewardship and smarter public policy.

Many inner city people have become accustomed to street robbery, burglary, and theft as part of their lot in life. They live in the hopeless cycle of protecting their children and their property from violent people who would harm their family. In some neighborhoods crime is so common that much of it goes unreported. By being accepted as a part of everyday life, crime loses its horror, and children get used to it as the injustice that is visited upon them for being who they are.

"Seventy-five percent of one thousand African-American elementary and high school students reported witnessing at least one robbery, shooting, stabbing, or murder . . . 72 percent of fifth and sixth graders in a southeast Washington, D.C. elementary school saw at least one act of community violence." (Trickett and Schellenback, *Violence Against Children in the Family and the Community,* **APA books, 1998, p 103.)**

In an Atlanta 1993 Survey for the CDC, 11.8 percent of ninth through twelfth graders carried a gun to school; 24 percent said they were offered an illegal drug; 7.3 percent said they were threatened or injured with a weapon while at school; 4.4 percent of the students skipped at least one day in the previous month because they felt unsafe.

There are few topics as explosive as gun control, but fewer still that generate the frightening statistics and newspaper headlines.

"Students carry an estimated 270,000 guns to school every day. In a study of first and second graders in Washington D.C., 45 percent said they had witnessed muggings, 31 percent said they had witnessed shootings, and 39 percent said they had seen dead bodies. In a study of eighth graders in Chicago, 73 percent reported they had seen someone shot,

> **stabbed, robbed, or killed."** (Crimes, Misdemeanors, and Violence Statistical Record of Children, 2003, p. 814.)
>
> **"Last year in Chicago police seized 10,509 guns. In that same year, about eighteen thousand inmates released from Illinois prisons came back to Chicago."** (George Will, "Money and Lives," *Minneapolis Tribune*, February 25, 2005.)

So many young Americans are using lethal force to settle arguments that should have been fistfights. Thousands of misguided poor American children kill and are killed, or are put into wheelchairs and comas because they have grown up in crazy homes with no means to make sensible choices. Guns and drugs are everywhere. The choices many of these children have are all bad.

- International handgun deaths 1996: Germany, 213; Japan, 15; Great Britain, 30; New Zealand, 2; and U.S., 9,390. The combined populations of Germany, Japan, Great Britain, and New Zealand are about 300 million people, compared to about 300 million Americans. An approximate population-to-population comparison would be about 360 handgun deaths for the combined nations versus 9,390 handgun deaths in America.

- In a typical year, over 30,000 Americans die of gunshot wounds. Almost three times that many are treated in emergency rooms for nonfatal gun injuries costing over $100 billion per year. In all, over three-quarters of a million Americans have been killed since 1960 in firearm-related homicides, suicides, or accidents. (John D. Bessler, *Kiss Of Death*, Boston Northeastern University Press, 2003.)

- A 2001 Child Welfare League study states "Firearm deaths of children in the U.S. are twelve times higher than in all the other industrialized nations combined; also that 66 percent of youth suicide attempts are with guns; over 80 percent of their attempts are successful."

- In the early 1990s, the U.S. had 285,000 gun dealers (more gun dealers than gas stations). (John D. Bessler, *Kiss Of Death*, Boston Northeastern University Press, 2003.)

- A 1993 Louis Harris poll about guns among American youth reports that one in twenty-five students carried a gun to school that month and 59 percent of them knew where to get a handgun if they needed one.

Does the ready availability of firearms in America encroach on our rights to live in a peaceful society? Is there a value we're sacrificing to have safe streets; gunfire free neighborhoods; property in the city without bars; or in a growing number of states, windows without big signs banning guns on the premises? Have we let policy makers create dangerous and fearful communities?

Call to Action

Study the issues and make an effort to vote the best interests of children concerning the use of firearms in your community.

Visit these websites for starters:

www.bradycampaign.org (Grassroots Gun Control Issues)

www.vpc.org (Gun Control Issues)

http://dmoz.org/Society/Issues/Gun_Control/ (Gun Control Issues)

TEN

Crime and Punishment

(Costly and Counterproductive)

Absolutely no good can come from creating millions of angry and unemployable twice-abused men.

I have been detained by police on at least a four occasions for my own bad behavior. Most of the time, the circumstances involved alcohol. Even when I had done stupid, thoughtless things, the officers seemed to want the most positive results to come out of the circumstances. In retrospect, it is so glaringly obvious how different my life is today, because police officers did not make my life miserable for what were minor stupidities.

At least one of my offenses would have been deserving of harsh treatment and a stiff sentence. I could easily have spent time in jail for my youthful indiscretions. In today's world, a criminal record could very well have interfered with my success in the licensed field I have earned my living at.

I know an African-American man who has worked very hard to have a family and build a life like normal people. He has a much harder time than other men do, though, because he has spent time in prison.

I am impressed with his intellect. I like him immensely as a person. It hurts me that he has been unable to procure a job that pays a decent wage or own a home. He knows he's a second class citizen. He struggles daily to keep his wife from drugs and alcohol. He goes to work every single day and works all the overtime he can get. He works harder than anyone I know does. He and his wife have been trying to save enough to buy his family a home for several years.

It's a real hard life. Not long ago, his wife got drunk and did something stupid, and they had a fight. He did not hit her, but she dialed 911 and he went to jail. He almost lost his job and he could have gone back to prison. It's a real hard life. If I were him, I might be a very bitter man. No one wins by punishing this man anymore.

- Minnesota spends 5.3 times more money per prisoner than per public school student. In 2003, *the U.S. ranked ninety-one in staff-to-student ratio in its public school system* (ninety other nations have more teachers per student than America).

- Juvenile arrests for murder 2001: California, 196; Wisconsin, 134. (Crime State Rankings, www.statestats.com, Morgan Quinto Press, Lawrence, Kansas.) The U.S. accounts for one-third of the world's total of persons sentenced to death for crimes committed while under eighteen. Since 1991, we have executed seventeen child offenders (more than any other nation).

- Since 1992, nearly half the states have expanded their lists of excluded offenses, lowered the ages of eligibility (for prosecution as an adult) *from sixteen to fourteen or thirteen*, or granted prosecutors more authority to transfer cases to criminal court. This is a fundamental policy shift from rehabilitation to retribution for children.

- The results for children in the prison system are statistically much less positive in all respects compared to the children in the Juvenile Justice System. A sixteen-year-old who enters prison has very little hope of ever leading a normal productive life.

- Only Congo, Somalia, Iran, and the United States executed juveniles as of 2004. Almost 80 percent of executions of persons executed for crimes committed as juveniles were American in 2003.

- European Union member states average 87 prisoners per 100,000 people; the United States averages 685 prisoners per 100,000 people.

- With only 4 percent of the world's population, America now has 25 percent of the world's prison population.

- Annually, America averages about 15,000 juveniles in adult prisons. About 20 percent of them were committed for property crimes, and 16 percent have been committed for drug or public order crimes. Over 20 percent of all violent crime victims are juveniles.

- Forty-four percent of African-American men living in Hennepin County (Minneapolis, Minnesota) were arrested in 2001. There were no duplicate arrests among them. In fact, 58 percent of these men went on to be rearrested for a second crime within two years. (African-American Men's Study, 2002.)

- Forty-eight percent of African-American boys dropped out of school in Minneapolis Public schools in 2002 (*Minnesota Spokesman Recorder*, "Special Ed: The New Segregation," Rosi Tavf, February 12, 2004).

Under President Clinton's watch, The Kingpin Laws, Mandatory Minimums, and punishment for growing small amounts of marijuana became the norm. Today sentencing guidelines demand that growers of small amounts of marijuana serve huge sentences. It is common that small marijuana grower face sentences two or three times longer than murderers. Over 50 percent of our prison population are non-violent drug offenders.

Under the 1980s Kingpin drug laws and the Mandatory Minimum Sentencing Act, high-paid attorneys for wealthy drug clients are able to have their client's sentence reduced by giving up those other people who are a part of the drug conspiracy. The sentencing is harsh and mandatory. The judge is not allowed to take into consideration any outside circumstances that might work in favor of the defendant.

Enforcement of the Kingpin drug laws includes imprisoning many lesser-involved folks and often a girlfriend who was only guilty of being in love with, or afraid of, a drug dealer. Many women are losing their futures, and their children, to the harsh one-size fits all mandatory minimum sentencing that locks them up for many years.

Politics of punishment have all but demolished rehabilitation and meaningful sentencing. Many federal and state judges have complained and some have resigned over the gross unfairness of harsh sentencing guidelines.

The race to punish drug users was a political movement that was pushed through Congress with no public debate, and it is an example of the poorest political stewardship this nation has ever seen. Two presidential studies, over twenty years, on the effects of illicit drugs recommended exactly the opposite approach. Instead, Congress determined that imprisoning anyone even remotely involved with drugs would be a better public policy than reaching out to citizens or their children.

Today, thousands of at-risk youth receive the same sentence, perhaps for simply driving someone who has been a party to a drug deal as the dealer. The poorest and the least able to defend themselves receive the longest sentences in our current court system. Draconian drug laws have decimated thousands of families, and legislation is still being passed to stiffen drug crime penalties.

Americans have agreed (by voting) that incarcerating vast numbers of poverty stricken uneducated people, mostly for non-violent offenses, is a better alternative than anything else we can think of.

Many felons will never vote again. A large percentage will never hold a decent paying job. Unemployment (or underemployment) keeps people from becoming a contributing member in their own community. Remaining on the outside of one's own community creates a sense of hopelessness and failure. This sense of despair explains America's high rate of recidivism (50–70 percent).

Mandatory minimum sentencing needs to be rolled back in favor of laws that reflect the actual involvement of the defendant and seriousness of the offense. A mountain of evidence has been gathered over many years, nationally and internationally, to indicate that social programs are much more meaningful and effective than prison sentencing for non-violent drug crimes.

Is it possible that a program removing non-violent drug offenders from behind bars and placing them in socially responsive programs designed to help build life skills and self-esteem would be less expensive, more productive, and a more ethical means of handling this problem? It would be a major shift in policy, and no doubt, a dramatic and painful transition period would follow. But can anything be worse than what we have been building for the past thirty years?

Today mothers, imprisoned victims through the gross unfairness of the kingpin doctrine, can lose any chance of raising their children. Because of minor involvement with drug dealers and users, these women are placed in prisons far from their homes and unable to even see their children because of the long distances. Rather than provide rehabilitation and opportunities, our institutions are destroying these families. It's costly and tortuous public policy.

Depression, hopelessness, the never-ending remorse, and the tedium of prison life spell the end of one more marginal person in our community. Their children are cast out into an overburdened state system that can never replace what might have been a fair and caring home life. Who decided that it is better to invest billions in prisons and so little for helping poor and uneducated women?

Poor children are likely to grow up as poor adults. They will earn less and find it harder to get work when they grow up. If they have mental disorders, and over half the children in the Juvenile Justice System have diagnosable mental illness, they are ten times more likely to graduate into the Criminal Justice

System. In 1998, the children in Child Protection Systems were 59 percent African-American.

Scare tactics don't work. Get tough tactics don't work. The trouble with boot camps, detention centers, and get tough programs is that they co-mingle violent children with other children who might easily be encouraged into better behaviors if they were simply shown better directions and provided some training.

Sending juveniles into adult jails ensures a more violent youth with a more advanced approach to crime and asocial behavior. Sophisticated criminals teach naïve juveniles in the finer arts of crime and violence. What else could happen?

For the last thirty years, we would rather build prisons than libraries or playgrounds. Public support for late night teen programs is lacking; however, we have tons of money for new detention centers and prisons. It is as if Americans do not value crime prevention, only punishment.

Statistically, we can see that countries with the lowest rates of poverty and illiteracy have the lowest crime rates. American attitudes, politics, and policies have consistently concentrated on punishment and a revenge mentality against people caught up in the system. The fact that the system is disproportionately hard on poor people and people of color has been minimized.

- America has 25 percent of the world's inmates. Recently surpassing Russia, we are now the most violent crime-ridden industrialized nation in the world. Of our population, over 7 percent are in criminal institutions, compared to less than 1 percent for the rest of the industrialized world, except Russia.

- November 8, 2004, Bureau of Justice statistics show that during 2002, eleven states increased their prison populations more than 5 percent; the leaders were North Dakota (11.4 percent) and Minnesota (10.3 percent).

- Eighty-four percent of women in the federal prison system are incarcerated for non-violent offenses. From the implementation of the Kingpin laws (Mandatory Minimums) in 1980s to 2002, the women's prison population grew by 800 percent.

- According to Amnesty International in 2002, 81 percent of all executions took place in just three countries: China, Iran, and America.

- "Scores of prisoners suffering mental retardation or illness have been put to death. In 80 percent of executions since 1997, the original murder victims were white. The report lists fifty cases where African-Americans were convicted by all white juries, each on showing a pattern of black juror exclusion by government prosecutors." (Amnesty International, 2002.)

- Juvenile arrests in 2001; California, 239,000; Texas, 180,000; and Florida, 127,000.

- Since 1973, death sentences have been given to 140 offenders for crimes committed as juveniles. In 1999, the U.S. executed ninety-eight juvenile felons.

- In studies done of death-row inmates, most inmates were severely abused as children, and many of them have parents who were significantly mentally impaired. The childhood abuse suffered by these men was extremely brutal and prolonged.

- "Of fifteen death-row inmates . . . majority of subjects came from families in which parents or stepparents threatened each other with extreme violence. In six of these cases these acts were homicidal." (Cicchetti & Carlson, *Child Maltreatment Theory and Research on the Causes and Consequences of Child Abuse and Neglect*, Cambridge University Press, 1989, p. 715.)

Over seven million Americans are now in the federal penal system; 4.8 million are on parole. Washington State has almost 4 percent of its population on parole.

Adding America's jail population, Juvenile Justice System population, and Child Protection System population to all the sons, daughters, husbands, and wives directly involved in these systems, results in a big percentage of Americans that are enmeshed in government agencies.

- Three of every four children murdered in the twenty-six top industrial nations was American. (Robin Karr-Morse, *Ghosts from the Nursery*, New York: Atlantic Monthly Press, 1997, p.14.)

- The cries for longer sentences and more prisons grow louder with each new election. Wisconsin has reintroduced the chain gang and forces its prisoners to wear stun belts. Misbehaving prisoners are electrically shocked for infractious behavior. I suspect that some guards will find it very tempting to punish those prisoners who have made it on to a guard's personal grudge list.

- One in every thirteen African-American boys will go to prison before he is twenty.

- One in six African-American boys will never graduate from high school.

- One in eight African-American girls will not graduate.

- One in three African-American girls will have a baby before she is twenty.

- The jobless rate for minority 16-19 year-olds is over 56 percent. (*Minneapolis Minnesota Spokesman Recorder*, August 19-25, 2004.)

- Fifteen to 20 percent of American juvenile offenders are tried as adults.

I have a friend (Phil) who realized how hopeless the job market was for ex-cons. He recognized that highly trained personnel are employed to weed out possible bad hires. Most of the ex-cons I know work for under ten bucks an hour. Phil created a company designed to provide meaningful work for those who needed it most.

His formula of building a food manufacturing facility with a crew of 50 percent ex-cons worked pretty well. I saw real pride in men who had finally landed a job that made them feel like a normal productive citizen. It was a great program and needs to be replicated on a larger scale. Most employers would rather not hire ex-convicts. Phil proved that it was possible and profitable to work with convicts.

It is very hard for ex-offenders to find meaningful work in America. Phil's program failed because of a food bacteria outbreak in the sandwiches he manufactured. It was a new and unpredictable problem that put him out of business. To my knowledge, there are few (if any) business programs that pay the wages and esteem building dividends that Phil's business paid.

Not many years ago, America lambasted China for its civil rights abuses of working convicts for ten cents an hour. Today, a convict in China makes about twelve cents an hour compared to eleven cents an hour paid to a Minnesota convict. About 50 percent of the prison population is African-American, while African-Americans make up under 13 percent of the general population.

Some in my community still think that "the Negro is still languishing in the corners of American society and finds himself an exile in his own land . . . an appalling condition" (Martin Luther King, "I Have A Dream speech"). Too much truth still exists in Dr. King's observation forty years after he made it.

To accept that states predict the need for prison space by counting the number of children in Child Protection indicates the impersonal standards that define America and differentiate us from the rest of the industrialized world.

Angela Davis writes about the tragic stories of abused children turned criminals and their lifelong struggle with crime, violence, and mental illness. "This place welcomes a man who is full of rage and violence. Here he is not abnormal or perceived as different. Here rage is nothing new, and for men scarred by child abuse and violent lives, the prison is an extension of inner life." (Angela Davis, essay, "Race, Gender, and Prison History," *Prison Masculinities*, Philidelphia, Temple University Press, 2001.)

A 2001 Human Rights Watch report on prison rape touched on the subject of sexual slavery . . . "is commonplace in the system's most dangerous prison units." Hundreds of reports have been written on the humiliating circumstances within this nation's crowded and under-funded prisons.

There is a growing trend for violence and sexuality and abuse in American prisons. Our prisons have become notorious for allowing prisoner abuse, so much so that we no longer classify prisoner rape or abuse as a crime. There is very little public concern for humane prison conditions or rehabilitation programs for criminals.

- Every third home under construction in America is behind bars. (Robin Karr-Morse, *Ghosts from the Nursery*, New York: Atlantic Monthly Press, 1997, p. 238.)

- In 2004, one in thirty-seven Americans will spend time in jail, up from one in fifty-three in 1974.

- "The world's trade in illegal drugs is estimated to be worth around 400 billion dollars (about the same as the world's legal pharmaceutical industry). In 2003, the Federal government will spend almost twenty billion dollars on its National Drug Control Strategy, and the state and local governments will spend another twenty billion dollars." (*National Drug Control Strategy Budget Summary 2003*, February 2002.)

- Department of Labor statistics show recent jobless rates for African-American men in Detroit, Philadelphia, Los Angeles, Houston, and New York City, at about 50 percent.

- This is about identical to the rate of formerly incarcerated African-American men (60 percent)in those cities.

Politicians have shifted the blame for social problems away from inequality, racism, and injustice and placed it on the immoral acts of bad people. Statistically it's apparent that we have made people of color the bad people. It's a great deal simpler to judgmentally mete out punishment than to address social failures. Too many Americans would rather put their energy into blaming and hating than caring and fixing.

Most of the industrialized world long ago came to understand that public safety is better served by a civilized approach to crime. Most crime is the result of impoverishment and mental health problems resulting from an abusive childhood that can be impacted by early intervention, therapy, and education.

- In the U.S., drug use has remained fairly constant these past ten years, even though spending on enforcement has doubled during that time.

- Prison spending grew five times as fast as spending for higher education according to a recent report examining prison growth in seventeen states . . . dollar for dollar, state and local spending on corrections increased more than twice as much as spending on education or health between 1977 and 2001 (Justice Policy Institute).

With the possibility that 10 percent of America's population will soon be institutionalized, leading the industrialized world in crime and violence, do we owe it to ourselves to reconsider how our current social policies are serving us?

- One out of three black men are currently in the Criminal Justice System.

- Six hundred thousand felons are released from our prisons annually.

- In America, millions of un-rehabilitated ex-convicts will cost our counties and states billions of dollars in crime, therapy, re-institutionalization, and the very real cost of lost production.

- One in seventeen of all African-American men are current or former prisoners compared with one in thirty-eight white men. African-American men make up over 42 percent of the men arrested for violent crime and serve longer sentences in general than white men.

- Forty-six American states have laws that take away voting rights of anyone serving time for a felony.

- Ten states take voting rights away permanently.

- Almost one and one-half million African-American men cannot vote because of a felony (almost 15 percent of the African-American male population).

- In Alabama and Florida, 31 percent of black men are permanently barred from voting.

  Source: Human Rights Watch *Losing the Vote* The Sentencing Project, 1998.

The Sentencing Project Group reports that 70 percent of those sentenced to state prisons were convicted of non-violent crimes. Drug offenders were 57 percent of federal prison inmates in 1999 (www.drugpolicy.org, 2004).

Drunk drivers kill over 20,000 Americans per year. Almost all drunken driving offenses are dealt with as misdemeanors, punished by fines and loss of driving privileges. Most drunken drivers are white. Very few prison sentences are given to drunken drivers who don't kill someone. In comparison, typical penalties for crack cocaine possession are commonly five years for a first offense. With mandatory minimums, fifteen to twenty years for a first time offender is not uncommon.

Crack cocaine is a poor person's drug. Crack draws a sentence many times that of powder cocaine.

Weldon Angelos, a twenty-five-year-old producer of rap records, was sentenced for a mandatory minimum sentence of fifty-five years for selling several hundred dollars in marijuana on each of three occasions and carrying a gun while selling the drugs. It is his first offense. Other sentencing guidelines: terrorist bombing intending to kill a bystander—twenty years; second-degree murder—fourteen years; kidnapping—thirteen years; rape of a ten-year-old—eleven years. (*New York Times*, "Long Term in Drug Case Fuels Debate on Sentencing," September, 2004.)

- A federal appeals court ruled six to five that Arkansas can force a prisoner on death row to take antipsychotic medication to make him sane enough to be executed (*New York Times*, February 2, 2003).

- The Georgia Board of Pardons and Paroles decided James Bowden, with an IQ of sixty-five, (twelve-year-old equivalent) was competent to be executed in 1986.

- In 1980, America had no private prisons. In 1995, we had 104. Never before had it been possible in this country to become rich by incarcerating other people, but now it is commonplace. The prison industry is a multi billion-dollar business with lobbyists and big-time financial backers.

- The ex-convict lobby is the same size it was in 1866 (there is no ex-convict lobby).

In Minnesota, the average prison term went from 33.9 months in 2001 to 45.75 months in September 2004. In an interview with Minneapolis *City Pages*, November 17, 2004, Dakota County Sheriff Don Gudmundson claims prisoners are getting longer sentences when they are way past their prime. He states, "They're no longer a threat to society . . . [they're becoming] geriatric wards." He also believes that "the mentally ill do not have a place in America . . . the number of people [in jail] on psychotropic drugs is huge."

From my own study, I would agree. It appears that the number of mentally ill people in prison is statistically similar to the number of mentally ill children and juveniles in the Juvenile Justice System (50 to 75 percent).

"The poor and the black have been the chief victims of the death penalty." Clarence Darrow observed that "from the beginning, a procession of the poor, the weak, the unfit, have gone through our jails and prisons to their deaths. They have been the victims." (Ramsey Clark, *Crime In America*, Simon & Schuster, 1970.)

- Texas has over 450 men and women on death row, and America executed 317 people from 1998 to 2001 (John D. Bessler, *Kiss of Death*, Boston Northeastern University Press, 2003, p. 17).

- The annual estimated cost of crime in the U.S. is between $1.1 trillion and $1.6 trillion. These figures are calculated using insurance figures, prison and judicial system figures, and for various crimes based on some real and some estimated valuations.

- The real average cost of a gunshot wound: $16,500.

- The estimated average rape or assault valuation: $70,000 to $90,500.

- The estimated average value of death: $1 million to $3 million.

Most of us would pay more than these figures to not have our children, friends, or other family members raped and murdered. The cost of crime in this country is much higher than the current estimates would have us believe. Think about it. The methods used in this calculation do not include the fear that follows a violent crime or the mourning for a lost spouse or child.

I know parents who wasted away and died early after the violent death of their only child (whom I went to grade school with). I also have two acquaintances whose daughters were raped and murdered. I went to school with one of those victims.

Add the cost of crime, incarceration, court systems, and painful human losses and tragedies to the very real cost of wasted lives that often stretch a person's full life span, and it can run into the many millions of dollars per child.

Try to understand the simple differences between:

- a person who leads a relatively benign life, who gets a job, has a family, and becomes a productive member of his/her community, and

- a child who is made emotionally and mentally unstable through years of living in a toxic environment and will inevitably *fail at education, fail at personal relationships, and fail at getting along in the normal community.*

"We have got to stop building prisons and start building our children." (Colin Powell, *National Governor's Conference,* Summer 2000.)

Because the problems with violence and criminal behaviors are poverty related and much more prevalent in the poorer African-American community, suburban voters tend to ignore the problem. White flight over the last forty years has left many of our cities with crumbling neighborhoods without a tax base to provide adequate services to their citizens.

- Alabama has re-instituted chain gangs and actually trucks in rocks for them to smash. It has recently returned to a policy of shackling its women prisoners during childbirth.

- Many states allow drugs and rape in their prison systems. The violence committed within prison walls soon finds its way out onto the streets of our cities.

Almost all crime in America is a result of the high rate of recidivism and our own unique child abuse prison feeder system. Recidivism in American prisons is consistently about 66 percent.

- Over 90 percent of the Juvenile Justice population have come out of the Child Protection System (Minnesota State Chief Justice Kathleen Blatz).

- Over 90 percent of the Criminal Justice population have come out of the Juvenile Justice System.

- Percentage increase, between 1986 and 1991, in the number of women in state prisons: 75 percent (result of the new Kingpin laws).

- Fifty-five percent of women in state prisons were convicted of drug offenses.

- Sixty-seven percent of women prisoners in 1991 had children under eighteen.

- Thirty-five percent of state prison inmates had an immediate family member preceding him or her in prison.

- Twenty-five percent of women in federal prison in 1990 were either pregnant or had just given birth.

- Fifty percent of men imprisoned in 1981 held jobs before prison.

- Nineteen percent of the same group held jobs after prison.

- 1,899 Americans died in 1970 from legal and illegal drugs; 29,866 Americans died from cirrhosis of the liver in 1969. (Dan Baum, *Smoke and Mirrors*, Boston: Little Brown, 1996.)

My accountant tells the story of the businessman who had $90,000 embezzled by an employee. When he called the suburban police, they told him there was nothing he (or they) could do about it.

The next morning he called the chief of police and explained the situation this way: "Had I called you from my retail convenience store and some young man of color had stolen a candy bar from me, you would have sent out a squad and had the perpetrator arrested." When he then asked the chief if this was how the law worked, the police arrested the woman.

America builds prisons with gusto. Politically, rehabilitation has become a non-issue. The public and our elected officials have chosen to eradicate rights, amenities, pride, and hope from people who find themselves in legal trouble.

Our culture has little forgiveness for ex-cons. Jobs are hard to find and many felons have lost their right to vote. Fitting in is not easy if you don't have meaningful work. Unable to find meaningful work, untreated mental health issues, and a sense of hopelessness, combine to hinder a smooth return to society. Americans have come to accept a recidivism rate of 66 percent as normal.

Call to Action

Study the issues and form your own opinions. Social policy for non-violent offenses combined with inadequate Child Protection policies have filled our prisons and made life more dangerous for all Americans.

Visit this website for starters:
www.famm.org
(Families Against Mandatory Minimums)

Investigate Families Against Mandatory Minimums. Attend a meeting or start a chapter in your community. Support reasonable laws on crime.

If you're really courageous, meet an ex-offender and find out what it's like, first hand, to reenter society after being incarcerated.

ELEVEN
Public Perception
(Working on Empathy)

Most of the families that I've experienced in Child Protection have mental health problems, chemical abuse problems, and family histories of abuse and neglect. I have yet to encounter a family that had only one or two incidents that brought Child Protection into their lives. Almost all my cases have had mental health issues. It is hard not to feel some empathy for the parents as well as the children.

The only time I remember actually crying in a courtroom was when I removed a child from a mentally challenged woman (Louise). It was an intimate setting at a table with the judge, a social worker, and Louise. She was a lovely woman struggling to have a normal life.

Louise didn't use drugs or alcohol, and she was boarderline able to care for her child. Her problems became more serious, as it became apparent that her one-year-old son was a special needs child, and Louise suffered from an inability to control her anger. She lived with a family that had agreed to teach her life skills. Louise just could not master the skills necessary for keeping her son safe.

Removing the child was the right thing to do. She went on to have other children, and I became a regular figure in her life. Over six years several other children were taken from her custody. I have never met a person who worked as hard as Louise did to learn the work of parenting or was more concerned about being a good parent.

Most of her problems had to do with the special needs of her children she was simply unable to address. I have never struggled as much with making these difficult decisions as I did with taking Louis's children from her. Her case kept me awake many nights.

It hurts me to hear otherwise good folks denigrate the tragic individuals who have their children taken from them. I don't think most of us would say the tough things we say, or think the mean spirited things we think, once we have come to know the misfortunate people who lose their children to the county. I have changed my views since I became a guardian ad-Litem.

When mothers do terrible things to their children, it is not generally because they are terrible people, and they need to be punished. Mothers do terrible things to their children because they are mentally ill or suffering from the same kind of abuse they are visiting on their children.

A tragedy occurs. A baby is found in a dumpster or a four-teen-year-old boy randomly shoots someone. The public is quick to seek justice. We are becoming a nation of very little empathy.

No matter that her stepfather abused the twelve-year-old girl for years, or that the boy was tied to a bed in a room and sexually abused by his father from the ages of three to seven. The public sees the highlights of the story on TV, but not the events that led up to it. The children involved in the TV story have histories that prompted the early pregnancy or random shooting.

Because so many of us accept snippets of TV coverage of complex stories as *the* story, we are unable to understand and evaluate what needs to be done to solve the problem that caused it. We don't take the time to investigate, and it's easier to assign blame than to solve complex problems. In some ways, we are treating the issue of child abuse like we treated alcoholism and clinical depression in the 1970s. We don't like to talk about it, and we would prefer not to know about it. This type of thinking ensures the issues will fester and get worse.

In the 1950s, before Social Security payments adequately supported seniors, older Americans were the neglected segment of the population living in distress and poverty. The media picked up on senior citizens eating dog food out of cans and living and dying under bridges.

Once public attention was brought to the plight of poverty stricken seniors, public outrage got the attention of lawmakers with great results. Over a five-to-ten-year period, people called their legislators, AARP became a viable lobbying arm, Social Security became a real safety net, and seniors were taken care of much better than before.

The public is not clamoring for more information about Child Protection, personal histories of the people involved, or the court system that manages child abuse. There is little media coverage of systems that work properly and do their jobs well.

There is substantial coverage when tragedy strikes and when systems don't work. The public is quick to seek justice and to place blame on the guilty. Afterwards, there is little investigation and few discussions about how we might improve the systems that caused the problems. There isn't much interest in the topics related to children's issues, so not much is reported.

Still, the under-reporting of fetal alcohol births and mental health issues of children within our schools and Justice System shocks me. The fact that the nation's schools reported an average dropout rate of less than 5 percent (U.S. Dept of Education, National Center for Educational Statistics) for many years, when actual dropout rates were six to eight times 5 percent, should outrage people. The fact that 50 to 75 percent of juveniles in the Juvenile Justice System have diagnosable mental illnesses should cause us alarm.

Was the media failing to report these important facts, or are we that uncaring about children's issues? Before I did this research, I recall seeing the high school dropout statistics (scandal) story reported on *Frontline* (public television) and in the newspaper. It is my observation that the average citizen is not concerned enough about children's issues to know, or want to know, about how to solve them.

Why the media have not shown up in the states where Child Protection has become open to TV, newspapers, and radio is a sad reflection on what matters to us as citizens.

We live in a fast moving and busy society that values shiny things and sports figures and doesn't give much attention to the broken parts of our communities. Until the pain is so great that it affects us in our suburban homes, we are too busy to address the issues.

The press has a fundamental obligation to attend to public issues, like dropout rates, mental health issues, and what happens in the Child Protection System. We must draw attention to the seriousness of the issues at hand. The statistics and stories of this very troubling part of our society must be brought to the attention of our policy makers.

Somehow, funding for education has become a questionable endeavor, rehabilitating criminals a waste of money, and mental health issues for abused and abandoned children are not worth discussing. Without public support for the issues, there is no discussion. If no one brings it up, it is not an issue and politicians avoid it.

By continuing to ignore the important discussion of public policy concerning courts, institutions, and the human beings within them, we undermine the very thing that has made America a great and powerful nation. We are an educated, motivated, and efficient workforce that has built the most powerful economic engine in the world. By ignoring this discussion, we are heaping huge costs and inefficiencies on top of policy failures that are socially costly and a great detriment to our quality of life and international respect.

We the public have become far more enamored by the personal habits of sports figures and rock stars than we are concerned with the people and events that rule our lives. As a nation, we have become bored with the mundane affairs that determine the quality of life in this nation.

What states do the best job at removing abused and neglected children and finding those children new homes? What states do a good job helping the parents recover and return their children to them? What states pay the least attention? With the absence of media coverage for the issue, who could possibly know? *The records exist, and we need to know.*

The reality is that most states need to invest more into training their workers and create greater resources for the children and families they deal with. Once they develop their programs, they will discover more difficult, disturbed, and medically fragile children who need help. States will also discover that investing in children pays big dividends for better schools, safer streets, and happier communities.

Surveys in Washington State reported that over 40 percent of children placed in foster care were born to mothers who abused alcohol or drugs during pregnancy. Drug-exposed children may now constitute a majority of all children in foster care. (Elizabeth Bartholet, *Nobody's Children*, Beacon Press, 1999.)

- Every year over two thousand babies are born to Minnesota mothers who are not high school graduates.

- The average IQ of a fetal alcohol child is sixty-five. Because there is no placental barrier to alcohol, if the mother has six beers, the baby has six beers.

Cocaine and crack cocaine also have long-lasting effects on the children born to drug-using mothers. The fetus cannot break the drug down and babies are often born premature. The good news is that we have great technology and the ability to keep preemies alive today, where we couldn't twenty years ago. The bad news is that it can cost two or three thousand dollars per day to keep the child alive. For over twenty years, a substantial percentage of inner-city childbirths have been either fetal alcohol or crack cocaine positive.

"In all likelihood, a major cause of America's high infant mortality stems from the millions of low-income adults without health insurance. Effective prenatal care, universally available in all the other industrialized countries, negates most preventable infant mortality. We do not."
(David Strand, *Nation Out of Step*, p. 20.)

More than half of poor working parents do not get any paid sick leave, personal leave, vacation, maternity or paternity leave from their employers. Unlike the rest of the industrialized world, there is no federal mandate in the U.S. for employers to provide them.

Call to Action

Research a children's issue that is important to you. Find and connect with an interested reporter in your community with the intention of raising public awareness about children's issues.

Become more knowledgeable than the reporter and make it your intention to help educate him or her about the issues you are studying. Do not concern yourself with immediate results. We are in this for the long haul.

TWELVE
The Richest Nation in the World
(With Third World Status For Children)

Nicollette, a twelve-year-old girl from New York, is one of many child prostitutes that "are mostly locked away because residential treatment programs specializing in the treatment of prostitutes under sixteen do not exist." (*New York Times*; "Finding a Future for a Troubled Girl With a Past," September 10, 2004.)

Incarceration is needlessly punitive and victimizes abused children like criminals. Easily intimidated, young girls lack the confidence or emotional/mental ability to escape the hardened pimps who have recruited them, and lead truly wasted lives.

> **"Youth are more likely to be victimized in the adult court system. Children who are held in adult prisons are eight times more likely than young people in juvenile facilities to commit suicide, five times more likely to be sexually**

> assaulted, twice as likely to be beaten by prison staff, and 50 percent more likely to be attacked with a weapon. The shift towards trying more children as adults raises basic concerns about fairness." (Children's Defense Fund, *State of America's Children 2001*, www.childrensdefense.org.)

California has a greater gross domestic product (GDP) than all but six nations. In 2001, California had a GDP greater than all but four other nations. In 2003, Minnesota had a greater GDP than Mexico, Austria, Poland, Saudi Arabia, Norway, Denmark, Finland, Turkey, Venezuela, and many other countries.

When we are discussing how to care for poor people, old people, young people, mentally ill people, it's not really about the money. We are arguably the richest nation on the planet, ever. Yet, children living in poor countries from Mexico to India are more likely to be vaccinated against major childhood diseases than they are in America.

While they may exist, I have not discovered any meaningful programs in my community for abandoned gay or lesbian youth or those neglected and abused children who have become child prostitutes.

It will cost us less if we choose to see that the Nicollettes of our community obtain the treatment and services they need to become *normal, functioning* members of our society than if we allow her to devolve into the life of drugs, crime, and poverty that she is now guaranteed. Her social costs, and the costs of her children and her children's children, will reach many millions of dollars in a short time.

According to *Minnesota Council on Foundations 2004*, (www.mcf.org), more than 90 percent of youth-serving nonprofits have been forced to cut staff, hours, programs, service levels, or quality. In the previous two years, more than 2,400 youth have been turned away from programs and services they once got from the nonprofits in the survey. Nearly two-thirds of the nonprofits reported a decline in government funding for their youth development programs in the previous two years and a drop in funding from foundations and corporate grant makers.

We have more conspicuous consumption in the U.S. than in any other nation in the world, but our child mortality rate, literacy rates, and per capita rates of incarceration have remained worse than most other industrialized nations for many years. It would be interesting to graph the international comparison of all the quality of life indices and see how many emerging countries (with a sliver of our GDP) were better able to care for their poor children.

Twenty-three industrialized nations have universal health care, paid maternal/parental leave at childbirth, and family allowance/child dependency grants (Office of Research, Evaluation and Statistics, Social Security Programs Throughout the World, *Summary Table and Individual Entries 1999*, August 1999).

According to Harvard College Project on Global Working Families, 2002, (www.globalworkingfamilies.org) many other nations have child friendly requirements that America has not adopted:

- Seventy-five other nations allow women to breast feed at work; the U.S. does not.

- Ninety-five other nations require employers to pay annual leave for illness; the U.S. does not.

- Forty-four other nations require employers to pay fathers parental leave for childbirth (www.globalworkingfamilies.org).

- Thirty-eight other nations allow for early childhood preschool enrollment programs; the U.S. does not.

- Bangladesh, Cameroon, Zambia, Brazil, Mexico, Finland, Norway, Sweden, France, Botswana, Denmark, and about 110 other countries offer working mothers between 25 and 100 percent of their wages as paid leave for twelve weeks or more upon the birth of a child. Mongolia offers seventeen weeks at 70 percent; Iran, sixteen weeks at 66 percent; and Canada, fifty weeks at 55 percent pay. One of very few countries (like Swaziland), the U.S. doesn't provide for paid leave for childbirth.

- The absence of health insurance coverage causes eighteen thousand unnecessary American deaths annually. (*New York Times*, Jan 12, 2005.)

- The World Health Organization "ranked the countries of the world in terms of overall health performance, and the U.S. was . . . 37th (Jeremy Rifkin, *The European Dream*, New York: Penguin Publisher, 2004, p 79)

In my work to research information for this book, it has become clear that the rest of the industrialized nations seek to include their entire populations for social programs and a better quality of life. Equally clear to me is the obvious policies of exclusion that are practiced in America that keep poor people from day-care, health care, early childhood programs, quality education, or many other quality of life programs that are available to the rest of the industrialized world.

It's hard to know which interest groups are fighting paid leave and universal insurance harder—business groups, politicians, or we the people.

Many low-wage workers lose their jobs when they take time off for the complications of childbirth. Lack of basic health care for poor children in America is a growing problem.

Call to Action

Understanding why children need pre-K education, health care, and parents able to provide basic necessities to thrive is a first step toward supporting badly needed social programs that accomplish these goals. Become an advocate for child friendly legislation. Get interested; get involved. Participate in, or send money to, a program you believe is addressing the issues.

Find out about positive quality-of-life programs in other states and other countries. It is up to those of us who know and care to bring these issues to the attention of the media and our politicians. Sensible legislation would clear away many obstacles to improvement.

Voting for child-friendly social programs gives a mom a chance to put her child in day-care. Paying day-care workers a livable wage would attract more talented people to the profession. End the underfunded and poorly run child care that is almost unique to America among the industrialized nations.

Don't accept the political argument that Third-World status is good enough for us. We deserve more. Stand and fight for your rights as a citizen. Send a letter to your state representatives and let them know you stand for the rights of poor people and children. Let your legislators know how you want your tax dollars spent. Americans should be able to enjoy the same luxuries as do people from Zambia, Mexico, and Cameroon.

Tell your legislators that you support child friendly programs.

Email Parents Action for Children:
info@parentsaction.org.

THIRTEEN

Supportive Networks
(Generations of Suffering and Dysfunction)

In times of serious family trouble, normal families fall back on mom, dad, grandma, siblings, or other relatives. Most of us have had the luxury of help from family, at one time or another, to make it through a bad experience. Without the help of family members who cared enough to reach out and provide a safety net in times of trouble, many more Americans would experience the severe consequences of mistakes and bad luck.

I have experienced the sadness and dysfunction of large families. With fifty relatives, not one could qualify to care for the children being removed from their crack-cocaine-using parents. No one in the family could help the terribly addicted parents get off the train of drugs and alcohol. One husband and wife went six months without producing a single clean urine analysis. The variety of drugs that showed up in their UAs was mind-boggling.

Generations of addicts and alcoholics exemplify the depth of the family's repeated cycle of inability to cope with life. One drug-addicted member is caught up in the net of Child Protection, and the rest of the family responds poorly and is unable to prove to the courts they can offer the child a safe new home. Once the cycle is broken, the children go on to lead normal lives (if they are removed from the home soon enough, and receive the necessary help).

These families had been dysfunctional for generations. Their relatives have serious problems with drugs and alcohol, abuse and neglect of their own children, and are, for so many reasons, a hopeless and inappropriate choice for the well-being of the child.

The cyclical nature of drug, alcohol, and child abuse is obvious to people who work in the system of Child Protection. Addiction is everywhere, and it is so destructive to the individual, their family, and especially their children. It would be an important and meaningful study to discover how many generations have been affected by addiction in each family within the Child Protection System.

Often we are unable to salvage the life of any given abused or neglected child. I have found it overwhelming to work with the intergenerational addictions of large dysfunctional families. It would be useful to determine a best practices approach to effectively deal with large dysfunctional families. Big dysfunctional families steeped in drug and alcohol abuse have a serious negative impact on their children.

At the same time, other families have super-committed and caring uncles, aunts, and grandparents who step forward into long-term foster care and adoption. I have been told by one elderly adoption resource grandmother, "when the youngest child is eighteen, I shall be eighty-eight years old."

Loving people, they are unable to watch the pain and continued punishment of their own grandchild from the self-destroyed parent—who once was their own child. Grandparents often step in with minimal resources, too old and too tired, but they are determined to make a difference in the lives of their grandchildren.

Often, their grandchildren are special-needs children who can be a terrific burden to the grandparents who are now quite stressed by having to relive parenting at an advanced age. It's important that our communities support these fine people in their efforts to raise and to save their grandchildren. The value they bring to the adoption and fostering of abused and neglected children is incalculable. They deserve the best resources we can afford to give them for their tasks.

Many sources show the value of mentoring and Head Start programs. Mentored youth are 46 percent less likely to use drugs, 27 percent less likely to use liquor, and 33 percent less likely to hit someone. Head Start statistics show 33 percent less juvenile arrest rate, 41 percent less violent crime rate, and a higher high school graduation rate.

The average salary of an American waitress is $194 per week. Many families are two wage-earner families who still cannot afford health care or day care. Many hardworking Americans have multiple part-time jobs without benefits.

Why is it that America is the only nation among all the industrialized nations to *not* provide universal health care for its citizens? Why is it the rest of the industrialized nations provide for early childhood education, and America doesn't? Do we not value all our children? In the 1930s, we created a safety net for senior citizens. Are our children any less worthy?

Our adult selves are the direct extension of our childhood years and the places we have lived. Scarcity, violence, and a cold, distant state for a mother can create a cold, hard, asocial being. We need to support children's rights like we support our personal rights, senior citizens rights, and our military.

Call to Action

If you know of anyone who has taken on the role of foster or adoptive parent, become a friend to him or her. Their issues are different. Your kindness will be appreciated. Do what you can to see that those adoptive parents and foster parents are supported within your community. It is the funding provided at the state and county level that determines the funding available to provide the services for the children they care for.

Make sure the people in the positions of power in your community care about these issues. If they don't, become active in replacing them with people who care.

FOURTEEN
Evolution
(What Have We Become?)

I have come to know many social workers in my guardian ad-Litem work. I am forever amazed at the terrific amount of energy they have for the children they work with. I have one worker friend (Ginny) who was treated very badly by her eleven-year-old state ward (Nancy). Even after eighteen months of being positively abused by this poor disturbed child, Ginny would smile and treat her ward as if she were her very favorite state ward child. I know that the terrible things said to her by Nancy injured my friend. It always hurts me to see unnecessary suffering.

It takes great strength to work with disturbed children. Part of the job description of social worker includes being stolen from, lied to, sworn at, and in many ways abused. Invisible Children are hurting, and they don't know how to lessen their pain. So the pain is transferred to the people around them.

I wish to thank every social worker who has had the desire and the courage it takes to be a friend and a surrogate parent to the often difficult and sometimes impossible children they work with.

We live in an age remarkable for its desensitization. TV and newspapers bombard us with the violence and distraction. We live in fear. Families in the poorer parts of the city talk about not moving from their chairs when they hear gunfire because shootings are so common. Children play indoors on beautiful spring days because they live in drug-dealing neighborhoods with fear and violence.

- Of all the industrialized countries, for many years America has ranked at or near the very bottom for lifting children out of poverty, child mortality, and child literacy. It is ironic that the most religious nation in the industrialized world maintains a great love for guns, capital punishment, gambling, and a tacit acceptance of policies that are so contrary to the well-being of its most vulnerable citizens.

- The U.S. is tied with Ecuador and Surinam for thirty-ninth in enrollment in early childhood care and education for three-to-five-year-olds.

- The U.S. spends about 4 percent of its GDP on social programs and has a child poverty rate of 22 percent. France and Belgium spend 10 percent and have child poverty rates below 8 percent. Sweden spends 18 percent and has a child poverty rate below 5 percent. America spends a much smaller percentage of its GDP on social programs than almost any other industrialized nation. We also suffer a far greater child poverty rate than most other industrialized nations.

Jonathon Swift (the Irish satirist/author) wrote an outrageous proposal to have poor Irish people sell their children at birth to make a nice stew for rich English people. He argued that it would save poor parents the pain of watching their children suffer in an unkind world, put money in their pockets, and provide the wealthy with a good meal. It was an awful satire at a time when most Irish babies were living and dying in poverty.

- Los Angeles, California, experienced almost fifty drive-by shootings a month in 1993.

- Seven million Americans are now in the federal prison system.

- Between one out of four and one out of six Americans are the victims of a crime every year.

- New York, Detroit, Compton, and Houston bear the distinction of having had between one out of two, and one out of three residents the victim of a crime in their cities.

Americans have become casual about brutality when it does not affect them directly. Avoiding these hard truths gives us no net gain. It is a costly failure to ignore the great suffering of these children and the adults they become. We are still proud of our get-tough-on-crime mentality. The rest of the industrialized world views our attitudes and statistics as outrageous and our social policies as uncivilized.

No ethical argument exists for not seeking rehabilitation, the execution of juveniles, or excessive mandatory minimum sentences for drug violations. We alone in the industrialized world feel that we have to be hard on criminals.

It is hard to predict the evolution of America and our standard of living based on the competition of emerging and first world nations. It is safe to assume that squandering the large and growing percentage our nation's gross domestic product, lost human capital, and the human suffering of crime and incarceration will hold us back and make us less competitive.

It is apparent that we are not competitive in quality-of-life indices as of today. Within five to ten years, the growth of the European common market, China, India, and the South American nations will all become much more competitive in the world markets.

These nations are dead serious about their positions in the world. The standard of living in these nations is tied directly to the efficiency and capacity to produce, as determined by the people who live here. If an unreasonably large percentage of Americans are living in institutions, costing the nation billions and producing nothing, we all lose.

A great many Americans are earning full-time wages that are below the poverty level. With the disappearance of long-term employment, very few poor or lower middle-class Americans will have adequate insurance or any retirement income other than Social Security.

Children bear the brunt of the growing cultural and economic disparities. For many years America has remained last, or near last, in lifting children out of poverty. Children born into poverty are behind their peers when they begin school in vocabulary and I.Q. Catching up demands an even playing field once they start school. We have not made educating poor children a priority, and we continue to pay the price.

Call to Action

Are your community and religious leaders speaking out for the weakest and most vulnerable among us? We need our churches, schools, state, and county social service agencies to reach out at a grassroots level to attract and provide for those children with the greatest needs.

Do your part to help get it done.
Visit: **www.invisiblechildren.org.**

FIFTEEN
Support and Abundance
(Starting the Dialogue)

My friend Pam and her husband (referred to in the introduction) were not told by the county that the three children they were adopting were seriously abused and neglected. The behaviors of these severely abused children quickly became unpredictable, violent, and frightening. The family worried about the potential for homicide or suicide by the oldest boy, and obvious sexuality problems with the two younger children.

There were many years of fear and sadness as these kind and decent people tried to sort out the issues (without understanding what caused them). In my experience, it is not uncommon for counties to withhold important information from adoptive parents.

Only years after the adoption was finalized did the children start to receive the mental health treatments they so badly needed. The treatments would have been much more helpful had they began at the time of the adoption. I watched my friend suffer prolonged mental anguish of not understanding the events in her life or knowing what to do about them. She is a strong and bright woman with a capable and supportive husband. They were both overwhelmed by the serious psychotic problems of the oldest boy and the ongoing problems with the girls.

Many communities are not set up to monitor sexual abuse cases or the mental health needs of state ward children. This makes it unlikely that they can make important observations and needed recommendations to adoptive parents.

Any government body that deceives its citizens, or actively works to transfer its problems onto individuals or other government systems, is a dishonest government, and it should be redressed for its actions.

Another example of bad public policy would be the states that buy bus tickets for homeless people to get out of town. Minnesota's Bus Ticket Forward program bought a one-way bus ticket for 4,500 homeless people to leave (forever) Minnesota. This type of policy exemplifies the extremes we the people will go to avoid caring for the weakest and most vulnerable people among us.

States and institutions need to comprehend that moving people from their state to another state *only exacerbates the problem*. Moving children from toxic homes to abusive foster homes or underfunded state facilities *only exacerbates the problem*. Moving children from Child Protection to Juvenile Justice *only exacerbates the problem*. Once the child has moved into the Criminal Justice System they have become a long-term and very serious problem with no easy or effective solution.

The answer lies in ending children's progression from the Child Protection System to the Juvenile Justice System and on into the Criminal Justice System. This is a core point of the book and the reason I speak on the topic.

Until our legislators take responsibility for the solutions-based approaches that will resolve our problems, we will have to accept the musical chairs approach of one-way bus tickets and public reaction to babies left in dumpsters that now define us as a nation.

> **"No state fully complies with Child Protection standards established by the federal government, . . . while some states have gotten national attention because of scandals in their child welfare programs, . . . sixteen states, including Minnesota, did not meet any of the seven standards that focus on children's safety and well-being." (*Minneapolis Star Tribune*, April 26, 2004.)**

Half-measures that try to compensate for the lack of funding and lack of understanding of children's mental health issues guarantee failure. Children with emotional and mental health problems are lost forever because they were unable to get the help they needed—when they needed it. Eighteen-year-old children with the mental development of a thirteen-year-old are headed for pregnancy or prison and a lifetime of poverty and suffering.

Half-measures in the training and funding of social workers and resources they need to do their work will also lead to failure. Social workers are committed people trying to make a difference in the lives of the people they work with. I've yet to meet a social worker who has entered the profession for any reason other than an honest desire to bring positive change to troubled families. We would all benefit by cultivating empathy for these children and appreciating the commitment of remarkable people who have chosen this field.

Without funding and community support, social workers remain under-trained and have their hands tied when trying to save abused and neglected children from their many problems.

When social workers are well trained and well supported, they can make a great difference in the lives of the children they work with. When they are not supported, what disappointing and thankless work it must be.

The Child Welfare League of America recommends caseloads for childcare workers be kept under fifteen families. Some systems are operating at over fifty families per worker. Since 1989, Illinois has paid almost eight million dollars to defend state welfare officials for not doing their jobs.

Their caseloads were too great because there were not enough workers to handle the work. With eight million dollars, the state could have hired two hundred childcare workers. Some communities find it easier to keep their head in the sand and pay fines rather than create better answers for their abused and neglected children. Think of the wasted money and unnecessary suffering.

If there ever were a place for training, support, and abundance, it would be to provide for the people who are taking the burden from the state and raising other people's children. This would solve many problems. There deserves to be at least complete training and support, if not some abundance, for these valiant people.

Our rich and fortunate community has grown compla-
cent. We have no roadmap to see where we will be in ten years.
From a humane perspective, we are not seeking happiness or
the elimination of unnecessary suffering. Like all grassroots
movements, children's issues must be talked about. The
dialogue has to occur before change can happen.

Call to Action

Music, dance, theatre, and art give children attracted to these
fields, a surrogate to close personal contact (love and trust),
and a place to express their feelings and passion. Several of my
guardian ad-Litem children have demonstrated superb talent
in the arts. It solves so many personal problems when children
discover self-expression and discipline in the development of
their own talents. Facilitating this development takes money
or creativity.

Here's a creative way to help children find a place to put
their passion:

> You will be surprised how many free pianos can be
> found in a church congregation if approached properly.
> Many adoptive or foster parents would put one to good
> use. Put an ad in your congregation's bulletin: wanted,
> unused pianos (in working condition) for adopted and
> foster children.

> Then, contact Child Protection in your commu-
> nity and let them know when people offer you their
> piano. I have also successfully contacted local banks
> to solicit donations that would pay for the moving of
> pianos. I have also found that music stores will move

pianos free if the cause is a good one. There are many generous people in your community. Find them and ask them to help. In Minnesota we use **www.pianosforkids.com** to list and distribute free instruments and lessons.

This approach works for all the arts. Creative people are, by nature, kind and generous. Make it your work to create a similar venue for other forms of music, theatre, dance, and art.

SIXTEEN
Fair Questions
(Possibilities)

For too many years American schools have under-performed against the rest of the industrialized nations. Twenty-five percent of American high school graduates are illiterate. As a volunteer reader in a metropolitan grade school, I worked with three illiterate third graders for one year. The program places an adult for one hour a week with a child who needs help with reading. Most of the other readers were senior citizens. I think even rest home seniors would have loved the work and been good at it.

It hurt me to listen to illiterate children with small vocabularies mispronouncing even small words on the printed page. At the end of the year, all three children were reading at grade level. I am convinced that the simple volunteer reading program and personal attention were all that was needed to create literate children. It may have been just as important for the child to have an hour of my personal time each week as it was to spend the time reading. Whatever the explanation, these children thrived with just a small amount of personal attention.

- Is there a great waiting pool of American volunteers just waiting to help children do better in school and live happier lives?

- Were public school teachers hired or trained to care for the multitude of disturbed children in their classrooms who are (or need to be) in the care of mental health professionals? Over 50 percent of the children in the Juvenile Justice system have diagnosable mental illness. Many states provide almost no mental health services for troubled youth.

- Do you expect that clinically untrained teachers do a good job providing psychiatric care to mentally disturbed students? Do you think that teachers are even aware of that part of their job description? Or, that the average teacher has a good grasp of the depth of the mental health issues these children are plagued with? Can they even begin to deal effectively with the psychosis and neurosis that affects some of their more disturbed students?

- Could it be seriously disrupting to the rest of their students and negatively affecting the school's overall performance to have two or three disturbed students in their classrooms? Are the majority of students under served because teachers are required to spend the majority of their time dealing with troubled children?

- Is it not probable that the continued failings of our public school systems are negatively impacted by political manipulation and distorted truths? Isn't it dishonest and counter-productive to blame the teachers, blame the administrators, and blame the immigrants?

- For many years, American public schools reported dropout rates at or below 5 percent when, in fact, their dropout rates were in excess of 30 percent. At a time when schools are being blamed for so many problems, who do you think was responsible for this distortion and why did it occur?

- Is it possible that the federal "No Child Left Behind" law was designed to wreck public education?

- Is it important to take the politics out of education?

- Is it significant that ten years ago thirty-seven out of one hundred adults of color were enrolled in college and today only twenty-six out of one hundred are? (*Star Tribune*, College, B1, September 15, 2004.) This is a factor of greater than a 30 percent drop in college enrollments for people of color. This is a significant sign that the communities of color need more, not less, attention concerning access to education.

- New Jersey has dropped its mental health services within its school system and is now incarcerating maladjusted and misbehaving students. Between 15 and 20 percent of those students are placed in adult jails where the statistical possibilities for a normal productive life are extremely slim. Children in New Jersey have been incarcerated for turning out the lights in a classroom (*New York Times*, "Unruly Students," January 4, 2004, p. 1). Is this a practical solution for the rest of the nation?

- Would we be better off fully funding education, paying teachers competitive salaries, equipping classrooms with sufficient current technologies and adequate supplies that would demonstrate a commitment to our schools?

- If schools are meant to be for the public good, how could privatizing them be any more useful than privatizing the police or military? Privatized systems concentrate on making money and certainly not on helping the weakest and most vulnerable children in the system. By definition, civilization seeks to lessen the suffering of the most vulnerable. By definition, the most needy would be left by the wayside by privatized educators. Can a long-term strategy for losing money be part of a business plan for a privatized education system?

- Adolescents and very troubled children are not easily adopted, and thus must be placed in long-term foster care or residential treatment facilities that cost $6,000 to $9,000 per month per child. Through the Doctrine of Imminent Harm and waiting a long time to take children out of toxic environments, are we creating more seriously disturbed children for the county to care for at very high costs with a much higher failure rate?

- Could it save our nation money if there were dental chairs and dentists within the schools who practiced preventative dentistry (as in Denmark)?

Reported by the *Minnesota Spokesman Recorder*, December 2, 2004, "In 2000, African-American boys accounted for 23 percent of the Minneapolis public schools" student body; however, they made up 37 percent of all students in Special Ed programs, and 55 percent of all students in programs for emotional/behavioral disorders." Data from the Minneapolis Research Valuation and Assessment of 2002 exposes the reading achievement gap that exists between African-American students and white students: 85 percent of white students passed the Minnesota Standards Basic Test (MSBT) reading assessment, while only 39 percent of African-American students passed.

- Have we undermined public education by berating its performance, underfunding its needs, and hiding its deficiencies until they are unbearable, all with the intent to dismantle a system meant for all citizens equally?

- Are jail cells a better investment than preschool education?

- Should the vast majority of people of color always be unemployed or earn 20 percent to 40 percent of the average white person's salary?

- Have the Draconian zero tolerance drug laws legitimized the incarceration of African-American men on a massive scale through selective enforcement of laws, permanently branding them as felon ex-offenders, and making them unable to find meaningful work at fair wages?

- Is there a social consciousness about the hopelessness of the drug laws and the increasing numbers of African-American juveniles diverted into a system of group homes and detention centers that reinforces antisocial behaviors which then leads to crime and imprisonment?

To not educate, not rehabilitate, or not instill hope in offenders creates a bondage to humiliation and defeat that ensures prison growth. It also ensures our communities' continued exorbitant investment in crime and punishment (and the minimizing of programs that actually work to reduce prison growth).

Have we made prisons a high growth industry offering big profits to entrepreneurs while undermining community efforts to reform this broken system? Can convicts or citizens lobby successfully against the well-funded prison-industrial complex, or are we doomed to a recidivism rate of 66 percent forever? Keep in mind, many ex-cons can't vote and they don't have a lobby.

The labor pool behind bars and recently released from prison in this country is the biggest cheap labor pool in the nation.

Call to Action

Fight legislation that bullies, imprisons, or punishes people for non-violent crimes. Ninety percent of the children in Juvenile Justice have come out of Child Protection. Over 90 percent of the adults in the Criminal Justice System are a product of the Juvenile Justice System. America has created a prison feeder system for abused and neglected children.

Legislators need to know how wrong their bad politics are and how many of us want humane policies. Become aware of legislative issues that impact the Juvenile Justice and Criminal Justice Systems. Work to soften legislation that incarcerates abused and neglected children.

Visit: **www.sentencingproject.org.**

SEVENTEEN
Where the Rubber Hits the Road
(Do Something, Even if It's Wrong)

Two boys on the seashore discover thousands of dying starfish with the receding tide. As the first boy bends down and starts throwing starfish back in the ocean, his friend says, "What are you doing, that's not going to make any difference." The boy with the starfish retorts, "Well it sure made a difference to that one."

About fifteen years ago I volunteered to help a Vietnamese refugee find a job. He spoke almost no English. At two hours a week, it took me about ten months to complete the task. A few years later he called me and asked if he could show me his properties.

His new found wages allowed him to purchase rental properties. Not only was he self sufficient, but he was building serious wealth and talking about the colleges his daughters would attend. For a few hours a week, I helped a man send his daughters to college.

Each one of us can have an impact without stretching ourselves. One phone call, one letter, one personal contact. Our efforts count. It is the only way change is made.

It doesn't take much to know more than your legislators do about these issues. Especially in times of budget shortages, legislators ignore issues that don't have public support. You and I must do more to create public support.

Invisible Children have no voice; they can't call their legislators. Very few people of either political party bother their legislators about neglected and abused children. Work to create a new framework in your community to evaluate and understand these issues. Whether from an emotional, financial, religious, or simple humanitarian perspective, what we are doing now is wrong and counterproductive. Change is waiting to happen. Become an agent for change.

Awareness building can be done by any of us. Our perceptions must find a way into our language and everyday speech. Some of us have time; others have ability or financial strength to support better answers and raised awareness.

For those willing to financially support people and ideas for change, remember to fund people who actually do good things, and not people who write grants. There is a difference. The secret to creating the greatest impact with your donations is threefold:

1. Determine the most pressing children's issues within your community,

2. Investigate the organizations or people that are addressing those needs,

3. Monitor the results of your donations and pay attention to the progress being made by the people or

organizations you are supporting. Maybe it is the woman down the block with the passion to bring change to her neighborhood.

Support the people who are trying to bring attention to pre-school education or parental training who could use some help being more organized and more effective. Pick a cause that resonates with you. As my mom used to say, "Do something, even if it's wrong." Change direction later if you need to; just start moving—now.

Organizations that have the most trouble getting started are those trying to change the system. Find serious, committed people working to make a difference, and give them money to shake the establishment tree. Institutions are dug in deep and not amenable to change.

Give to groups that inspire you. Fund people whose work is their passion. Give to groups that are creative and often doing unpopular things. Our nation is reaching a tipping point on how it treats its weakest and most vulnerable citizens. Do your part to push it all the way over.

People who are closest to the issues, like police officers, social workers, and teachers, are engulfed by their work and enmeshed in the systems. For them it can be hard to be objective. They may also find it difficult to fight a system that makes the rules they live by. That's why those of us who have the means need to engage our lawmakers and demand the creation of effective social institutions.

Small efforts by many people who are willing to be involved, demanding reasonable public policy, are the only way our nation can again become a leader in quality of life indices among the industrialized nations.

Many abused and abandoned children gravitate toward music, theatre, and the arts. It is my sense that a harsh past leaves a great void in a child that can be helped by the beauty and passion of music and the arts. The creative arts can give them a place to put emotions and passions that they can't put into people.

If you are in the arts, consider developing a program or ground swell movement to bring disadvantaged children into contact with the arts. Churches and other community organizations are a terrific resource to acquire donations of musical instruments and other items. Volunteers are everywhere; free pianos and theatre tickets are everywhere. Tickets to arts events can become free when someone has the time and energy to ask for them. Help set up a clearinghouse within your community for donated arts related things. Take a child to a play, dance, or musical event.

The Salvation Army has a terrific family-to-family program where life skills are transferred from successful sharing families to poor struggling people. These are the parents who didn't finish high school, who need to learn important skills to get by in this society. These folks often pay slum landlords exorbitant rents in crappy inner city tenements that could easily make a house payment on a nice home if only they had the outside mentoring to help them make better choices.

Programs exist that help people make better choices. Many renters are simply too busy, too unaware, and too stuck in their negative paradigm to make it happen. Find, or create, a program that leads the way. It could be taking a few hours a month to help someone better understand the options and take advantage of programs that might help them improve their living conditions.

Find out about guardian ad-Litem programs in your community. Learn how Child Protection works in your community. Are the workers trained well? Are caseloads reasonable? Each county has a system based on the funding available through the state and county. Some counties are well funded with well run systems and adequate resources. Other counties are seriously underfunded and poorly run.

Talk with the judges, therapists, educators, and law enforcement agencies in your community. Ask their opinions about how they assess the quality of Child Protection in the community. Find out what they think needs most improvement. Do they believe that the county and state institutions work together when dealing with issues of child abuse? Is there concern and coordination between the institutions and efforts to mitigate the harsh legal consequences that make the end results of child abuse so permanent and so devastating?

In some communities social agencies do not work well together. It would be a good thing if more attention were drawn to what can be done to make them more successful in getting better results with abused and neglected children.

Here are several areas I have witnessed that need attention in most Child Protection Systems:

- In your Child Protection System is there a volunteer program from a local law school that assigns a volunteer attorney to an abused child? I've met some well-meaning and bright attorneys who genuinely care for their clients this way. If not, are there adequate public legal representation for abandoned children?

- Does an appointed attorney (for the child) receive the call when the child gets into trouble outside of

Child Protection? Or, does some other unknown lawyer who knows nothing of the child or abusive background, therapy, drug regimen, or mental health issues? There are many pieces to this puzzle that need to be discussed and thought through.

- Gay and lesbian issues are very uncomfortable for many of the people in Child Protection and the Juvenile Justice System. Because of this, GLBT issues are often ignored to the serious detriment of Invisible Children. I live in a pretty progressive metro area, yet it does not have much to offer gay and lesbian children in the system. Most child workers have been slow to recognize, and slower to address, sexual identity issues (even with me advocating for the "right" thing).

Children who have all the mental health problems of being abused and abandoned, who also have sexual identity issues, can pretty much expect to be treated as badly by the county as they will be in the rest of the world. We solve nothing by avoiding critical issues. The pain of avoidance is felt by the child and later our communities.

Those of us who understand and care about these issues need to better explain them to our less informed friends and neighbors. Being silent has not done these children (or us) any favors.

"At issue is what kind of state and country we want to be. Do we ignore children's needs and then react when they become a burden to society, or do we put all the resources we can into them and plan for an enriching future? It's

**time to put our money where our future is—
and children are our future. The greatest goal
we can set as a society is to ensure our kids show
up at kindergarten nurtured and ready for life"
(Dennis   Benson,   Warden,   Minnesota
Correctional Facility at Stillwater).**

Have you ever read or talked to a prison warden or other
justice official in your state? Many people in the Justice System
have eye-opening recommendations for how communities
might better address issues. Many communities have bright
and capable professionals trying to make a positive difference
in regressive state and county systems. The Internet now allows
us to find out what important community figures are doing
and recommending. Take advantage of what is available and
support those people you believe can help bring change to
abused and neglected children.

Young people who have mentors are more likely to graduate from high school, enroll in college, and be hopeful
about the future. They make better parents and don't have
the serious problems with drugs, alcohol, and crime that
non-mentored youth do. Mentorship programs are easy to
start. It really only takes a mentor. If this appeals to you, find
someone in your community who has mentored a child and
learn from them. Whether you mentor a single child or begin
a mentoring program within your community, you will be
making a difference.

**"For every child, a home and that love and
security which a home provides and for that
child who must receive foster care, the nearest
substitute for his own home. For every child,**

health protection from birth through adolescence . . . a school which is safe from hazards, sanitary, properly equipped. For younger children, nursery schools and kindergartens to supplement home care. For every child, a community which recognizes and plans for his needs, protects him against physical dangers, moral hazards, and disease; provides him with safe and wholesome places for play and recreation; and makes provision for his cultural and social needs. For every child these rights, regardless of race, or color, or situation, wherever he may live under the protection of the American flag." (Herbert Hoover's 1930 Conference on Child Health and Protection.)

There are too many American children for whom the above mentioned conditions do not exist.

Call to Action

Places to learn more, contribute, or participate:

Cultivating a nation of neighborhood philanthropists:
www breadforthejourney.org (415-383-4800)

Network of community-based foundations:
www fex.org (212-529-5300)

Web based donations of musical instruments (Minnesota):
www pianosforkids.com

Minnesota guardian ad-Litem program and donations for Invisible Children: **www.friendsofchildren.com**

Minnesota mentoring programs:
www mentoringworks.org

National guardian ad-Litem program:
www.friendsofthechildren.com

Visit Salvation Army, United Way, your community churches. Bring children's books to your county's Child Court and Juvenile Justice system, and ask if you can warm up the waiting areas with free books for kids. Ask libraries to donate used children's books for a good cause.

EIGHTEEN
The Guardian ad-Litem Program

Not every community has a guardian ad-Litem (GAL) program, but they should. Champion a program in your community. Children need a voice in the Child Protection System. Social workers are wonderful, but the child needs an advocate in our complex legal system. One paid and trained Guardian staff person can manage up to fifty Guardians.

One Guardian can work with many children. Guardians can add a great value to your community and its children. Push to make it possible that Guardians can do more than just advocate for kids in court. I have kept enduring relationships with several of my young charges, six and eight years to date, with a possibility of being in their lives forever.

My volunteer part time efforts have had a powerful effect on the lives of many of the children I have worked with. Much of what I have been involved with has been successful and greatly rewarding. Even when I've been less than satisfied with the results, I know the child benefited from my presence.

The guardian ad-Litem program needs support in most states. Many communities don't have much of a program at all.

Children deserve an unbiased voice in the court system. The child's life is being decided and managed by a county, instead of a parent. Training social workers to do a parent's work is impossible. The best we can hope for is a fair effort. During budget shortages, this difficult task becomes even more complex and unmanageable. Invisible Children need all the help we can give them.

Guardian programs have many volunteers of all age groups and backgrounds. Potential volunteers are waiting to do their part for your community.

A GAL program provides so much to those who need it so badly and should be embraced by every county in every state.

Being a guardian ad-Litem volunteer can take as little as a few hours per week or as much time as you have. A few hours a month spent with an abandoned child can make you the most familiar adult in that child's life. Some children lose all contact with family after being removed from the home. Five foster homes and fifty social workers later, they have NO friends, NO family, and NO adults in their life. You could be it.

So raise your awareness and cast your vote for the boat of hope. If you have a friend, family member, or neighbor who needs direction in his/her life, maybe successful, maybe retired, maybe just tired, tell him/her about the issues. Do anything, even if it's wrong (at least you'll be trying—thanks Mom).

To form a ground swell movement in your state;
www.invisiblechildren.org
Our website will direct you to other places to go for
information and unique programs.

Visit: **www.friendsofchildren.com** to investigate the
guardian ad-Litem program or donate money for Minnesota
kids, or **www.friendsofthechildren.com** to see the national
guardian ad-Litem website.

EPILOGUE

Knowing what needs changing, and creating change, are clearly two different things.

These facts are not acts of God. They are our moral and political choices as Americans. We can change them. We have the money, the power, and the know-how. Why don't we?

It is the habit of getting involved that brings change. The habit of non-involvement works against change. *We the people* need to become comfortable participating as active citizens and to make an effort to bring change. Without effort, there is NO change. Without change, our institutions will continue to exacerbate the problems and the results will continue to disappoint us.

Children with simple troubles won't get stuck in a well-run Child Protection System. These systems need funding for training and funding to assure workers are not overwhelmed with cases. Each of us can make our voices heard by enlightening our legislators. When children get stuck in Child Protection, they are there for a reason. Children's issues are beyond politics. Civil societies need protection for the weakest and most vulnerable among us. Children deserve a safe place in our society.

Recognize and appreciate the many committed people who try so hard to make the lives of these children better. Millions of us are out there. It's up to us to organize, speak out, and push for change. Show support for teachers, social workers, judges, and administrators when you get the chance.

Too many Americans live and work each day in a chaotic and negatively charged atmosphere that could be improved with better social policies. Schools, courts, and Child Protection Systems need our attention and awareness; the rest will take care of itself.

Terrible conditions endured by senior citizens in the late 1940s and early 1950s, compelled citizens to call their senators, form AARP, and change laws that would secure changes that made a better life for senior citizens. The same things need to happen to secure change for abused and neglected children today.

Seniors of fifty years ago could speak for themselves, and they did. To a large degree, they got their own results.

Unlike the seniors, these children cannot speak for themselves. They can't tell anybody about the tragedies that are their lives. Often they don't know that the lives they are living are toxic and abnormal. No book is given to a child at birth explaining abuse or where to go for help.

Invisible Children need us, and we must speak out for them. If the citizens of this nation don't speak for them, there will be no discussion besides the mean spirited political rhetoric that exists today. Prisons, crime, failing schools, and poverty will become much less problematic as soon as a few enlightened citizens bring attention to what needs to be done.

What's missing for abused children are those things the rest of us have in abundance and can well afford to give away—kindness, trust, and a humane approach to solving problems. We are not short of the economic resources to make these changes. We are short of will. Our political will has been to turn up the punishment until the situation improves. It hasn't worked.

This book sparks a grassroots effort that needs a fire lit under it. Here's a match. When enough of us tell our friends, call our legislators, or make some small effort, we will draw attention to the steps that will change the lives of Invisible Children (and their children).

In a better world, courts will no longer condemn juveniles to the certain failure of the adult Criminal Justice System. It will recognize abused children are not to blame for the pain and suffering heaped upon them. No more executing of people who have committed crimes while they were juveniles. Some other mechanism will be found to deal with juveniles who have lived in putrid surroundings and become insane because of it.

For two cents a day from each American, we can convince our legislators to vote to vaccinate all of our children until the age of two. We will agree to spend the fourteen cents per day to insure the 9.2 million children who have no health care coverage today.

Libraries and the Internet provide a growing wealth of studies and comparisons between communities, states, and nations. Don't let yourself be confused by political rhetoric. As a First World nation that has Third-World status in most of the areas that determine the quality for fully half of its citizens, we need to recognize the trends, speak out and make some changes. Good people don't tolerate this kind of social injustice.

There are many complex issues that need addressing within each of our social institutions. There are no quick fixes. We will need to think our way through each problem. It is a good thing to be confused at a higher level. It is a positive step to have the discussion about our options and what other states and nations are doing.

Don't be paralyzed by the complexity or number of the issues that need attention. Instead, learn about one area of concern and make some tiny difference. Become (or organize) a Big Brother/Big Sister, guardian ad-Litem, Salvation Army family, United Way program, or give money to some worthwhile child-friendly organization that passes your smell test.

Some of us are better at rabble-rousing than others. Grassroots organizations can catch fire and bring about great changes in your own communities. The fires will spread.

For instance, if you agree with the serious problems I raised about abused and neglected children's impact on the school system, then learn enough about it to be taken seriously by your friends; and, by all means, tell at least one government official who needs to be educated.

You will soon discover that you know more about children's issues than your friends or elected officials. Very few politicians have even a basic appreciation for the problems teachers are facing with abused and neglected children in their classrooms.

Most teachers aren't aware of the number of abused and abandoned children in their classrooms or the seriousness of the mental illnesses the children bring to school with them. Most teachers don't dwell on the fact they did not become educators to provide services to neurotic and psychotic children. They just do their work. We as a community owe them a chance to succeed in their classrooms by supporting and fully funding education and the programs that will make educating troubled children possible.

I would argue that saving money on education is ridiculous in a nation that needs educated people so badly and that spends as madly as it does on prisons and the military. Ours is the largest and most expensive military in the world. Ours is the largest prison population with highest rate of incarceration in the industrialized world. In our schools, we rate ninety-first in staff-to-student ratio among all the nations in the world. In my state, there are 4.5 offenders per staff member in the prisons, thirty students per teacher in the schools, and growing in the wrong direction.

Bringing attention to educational and mental health issues is an uphill battle. Mental health issues are complex and poorly understood by the general public and many professionals. Because the public ignores mental health issues, the media avoids it. Because the media does not report it, even the social workers, teachers, and school administrators who are close to it lack the understanding to explain its importance. Mental health issues need more public discussion to raise understanding and shake off the stigma that today keeps the subject minimized.

Worse, educators have bought into the claims of politicians and the media that our problems stem from poor personal efforts, immigrants, and other political red herrings, instead of seeking to understand the complicated social and institutional failures that are responsible for the chaos in their classrooms. We need honest discussions and better stewardship to solve these problems. Twenty years from now, current trends will have dragged our nation from its comfortable status to more Third-World comparisons and more unbearable conditions for educators, social workers, citizens, and people forced to live within our nation's cities.

Find programs that work, then use them. Identify and avoid programs and ideas that don't work. A huge social saving will be realized as our communities move in the right direction. It all sounds so simple. It takes a thoughtful and informed citizenry to make better decisions to bring about badly needed changes.

Concerned citizens must make a stink about mental health issues, Ready 4 k programs, Head Start, and other core policies required to address truly needy children, and demand the support and financing to make them work.

Social policies that produce repeated generations of damaged children, whose lives are as tortured as their parents, must be replaced with more thoughtful and effective policies that are motivated by a genuine concern for a better society.

Misguided political leaders need to be identified and brought to task for their lack of understanding and poor stewardship. Through their artful use of language, politicians have led us to think we are voting for reasonable policies when, in truth, we have been hoodwinked into supporting failed programs and terrible policies. We need to identify and stop the outdated politics that make life even more miserable for people among us who have always had the least and suffered

the most. There are no benefits to the bac
brought us to this point.

> **"Other nations who don't have**
> **similar burden of poverty as the U.**
> **a substantial economic advar**
> **economic expense of providing support for a**
> **large portion of the able population . . . places**
> **too great a marginal strain on the productive**
> **workforce . . . In this task the child welfare**
> **system should play a major role. The child**
> **welfare system in modern market economies**
> **is responsible for ensuring opportunity for all**
> **children. When the child welfare system fails**
> **to protect children's economic futures, the**
> **long-term consequences for the nation are the**
> **burden of supporting a large welfare class,**
> **increased need for residual services for such**
> **problems as drug and alcohol abuse, delin-**
> **quency, and teenage pregnancy"** (*The Welfare*
> *of Children*, Duncan Lindsey, Oxford
> University Press 1994.)

We need to see far enough into the future to know that spending money on babies and children is a sound social investment. Reasonable people understand that on all levels, kindness and a desire to help people succeed bring better results and more happiness than denying people fundamental rights and the means to improve themselves.

It is our collective and individual responsibility to protect and nurture the weakest and most vulnerable among us. Americans are a wealthy and good-natured people. We can

ord to reach out with good intentions and create a better
rld for those among us who need our help.

Americans can create a better world because we have the
resources to do it and ethics rooted in individual morality. A
practical and optimistic people, we love life and know how to
make change occur. Getting a grasp of the subject and making
it our intention to create change is what is needed.

We are complex beings with poorly understood social
structures and institutions. Taken apart and viewed in pieces,
interpreting the inter-relatedness between our policies and
policy outcomes will bring clarity to what needs to change. It
will not be that difficult once public attention becomes focused
on the right issues and becomes attentive to what the better
answers are.

The results we are experiencing within our communities
are not deliberate, they are not an accident, but they are inevi-
table. The data and stories in this book are the acts of America's
political will. When we want something to happen, we will
make it happen. Policies are changed by one vote, one citizen at
a time.

Our system of participatory democracy is meant for this
type of challenge. The key is that each citizen has some obligation to participate. Because much of the population will not
participate, it is critical that those who can get involved do
their part, or a little more.

THINGS YOU CAN DO NOW

Call, write, and visit your government officials and educators and share your insights. Let them know there are better answers. Stand up and tell them it is time to invest in the lives of poor and abandoned children.

Work in your community to reach out and help Invisible Children live among us as productive and healthy citizens.

Visit our website:
www.invisiblechildren.org

Use our ongoing web dialogue to post
your interests and findings:
www.invisiblechildren.org/weblog

Share this book with other concerned people.

Send this book to people that you know should read it.

Send this book to your government officials.

Most importantly, be active and concerned for the abused and neglected children in your community.

Thank you,
Mike Tikkanen

BIBLIOGRAPHY

Barber, Benjamin R. *Passion For Democracy*. Princeton, New Jersey: Princeton University Press, 1998.

Bartholet, Elizabeth. *Nobody's Children: Abuse and neglect, foster drift, and the adoption alternative*. Boston: Beacon Press, 1999.

Baum, Dan. *Smoke and Mirrors*: *The war on drugs and the politics of failure*. Boston: Little Brown, 1996.

Bessler, John D. *Kiss of Death*, Boston: Northeastern University Press, 2003.

Califano Jr., Joseph A. "The Least Among Us," *America*, Jesuit Press, April 24, 1999. www.americapress.org.

Cicchetti, Dante, and Carlson, Vicki. *Child Maltreatment: Theory and research on the causes and consequences of child abuse and neglect*. New York: Cambridge University Press, 1992.

Clark, Ramsey. *Crime In America.* New York: Simon & Schuster, 1970.

Davis, Angela. Essay in *Prison Masculinities*, Philadelphia: Temple University Press, 2001.

Hoffman, Allan, *Schools, Violence, and Society.* Connecticut: Praeger Publishing, 1996.

Karr-Morse, Robin. *Ghosts from the Nursery*, New York: Atlantic Monthly Press, 1997.

Lasch, Christopher. *Culture of Narcissism*, New York: Norton Press, 1991.

Lindsey, Duncan. *The Welfare of Children*, California: Oxford University Press, 1994.

Postman, Neal. *The End of Education*, New York: Knopf, 1995.

Rifkin, Jeremy. *The European Dream,* New York: Penguin Publisher, 2004.

Rolnick, Art, and Grunewald, Rob. "Early Childhood Development = Economic Development," *Fedgazette,* March 2003.

Trickett, Penelope K., and Schellenbach, Cynthia J., *Violence Against Children in the Family and the Community.* Washington D.C., American Psychological Association, 1998.

Additional Reference Materials:

Centers for Disease Control and Prevention: www.cdc.gov

Child Welfare League of America: www.cwla.org

Children's Defense Fund: The State of America's Children: www.childrensdefense.org

Encyclopedia of Crime and Punishment, Sage Publications, Inc., California, 2002, www.sagepub.com.

FBI, Crime In the U. S., Uniform Crime Reports: www.fbi.gov/ucr/ucr.htm

Harvard School Of Public Health, Project on Global Working Families: www.hsph.harvard.edu

The Legal Action Project (of the National Committee for the Rights of the Child, Defense for Children International, National Court Appointed Special Advocate Association CASA: www.nationalcasa.org

Minnesota Spokesman Recorder, Minneapolis, Minnesota: www.spokesman-recorder.com

National Commission to Prevent Infant Mortality, *Troubling trends : the health of America's next generation*, Washington, D.C. : The Commission, 1990.

Report: *Handle with Care: Serving the Mental Health Needs of Young Offenders, Getting It Together, the Health and Well-being of Minnesota Youth.* Printed by the Coalition for Minnesota Juvenile Justice.

U.S. Bureau of the Census, Statistical Abstract of the U.S:
www.census.gov/statab

U.S. Dept. of Justice, Office of Juvenile Justice and Delinquency
Prevention: www.ojjdp.ncjrs.org

Additional Reading;

Bernstein, Nina, *The Lost Children of Wilder, The epic struggle
to change foster care.* Pantheon Books, 2001.

Courter, Gay. *I Speak For This Child, true stories of a child
advocate.* New York: Crown Publishers, 1995.

Hubner, John and Wolfson, Jill. *Somebody Else's Children: The
courts, the kids, and the struggle to save America's troubled
families.* Crown Publishers, New York, 1997.

Kagan, Richard. *Turmoil to Turning Points, Building hope for
children in crisis placements.* New York: W.W. Norton,
1996.

Other Useful Websites Referred to in This Book:

www.aap.org (American Academy of Pediatrics)

www.aacap.org (American Academy of Child and Adolescent
Psychiatry)

www.aclu.org

www.ahomewithin.org (A Home Within)

www.bradycampaign.org (Grassroots gun control issues)

www.bwjp.org (Battered Women Justice Program)

www.bwss.org (Battered Women Support Services)

www.cartercenter.org (The Carter Center Mental Health Program)

www.cwresource.org (National Child Welfare Resource Center for Family Centered Practice)

www.drugpolicy.org

www.endabuse.org

www.famm.org   (Families Against Mandatory Minimum Sentencing))

www.friendsofchildren.com (Minnesota Friends of Children)

www.friendsofthechildren.com (National org)

www.globalworkingfamilies.org

www.house.gov   (U.S. House of Representatives)

www.Mentalhealth.samhsa.gov (Mental Health Services for Children and their Families)

www.mentalhealthscreening.org (Screening for Mental Health, Inc.)

www.nimh.nih.gov/healthinformation/childmenu (National Institute of Mental Health) www.pcamn.org (Prevent Child Abuse Minnesota)

www.pianosforkids.com (MN)

www.preventchildabuse.org (Prevent Child Abuse U.S.)

www.savethechildren.org

www.senate.gov (U.S. Senate)

www.statelocalgov.net (Internet Directory for State and Local Government)

www.vpc.org (Gun control issues)

ABOUT THE AUTHOR

Mike Tikkanen has owned and operated an auto recycling business, garment manufacturing business, and a small business consulting firm since graduating from Moorhead State University in 1974.

Researching issues that impact children has been a part of his life for many years. He entered the Child Protection System as a volunteer guardian ad-Litem in the mid 1990s. Mike's book and public speaking are his efforts to bring public attention to core problems that are impacting schools, health care, crime, and quality of life for many Americans.

Mike Tikkanen lives in Minnesota with his best friend and wife, Cathy.